W9-BAL-212

Astronomy

Understanding Celestial Bodies

Astronomy

Understanding Celestial Bodies

Edited by Samuel Kazlow

Britannica
Educational Publishing

IN ASSOCIATION WITH

ROSEN
EDUCATIONAL SERVICES

Published in 2015 by Britannica Educational Publishing (a trademark of Encyclopædia Britannica, Inc.) in association with The Rosen Publishing Group, Inc.
29 East 21st Street, New York, NY 10010

Distributed exclusively by Rosen Publishing.
To see additional Britannica Educational Publishing titles, go to rosenpublishing.com.

First Edition

Britannica Educational Publishing
J. E. Luebering: Director, Core Reference Group
Anthony L. Green: Editor, Compton's by Britannica

Rosen Publishing
Hope Lourie Killcoyne: Executive Editor
Samuel Kazlow: Editor
Nelson Sá: Art Director
Brian Garvey: Designer
Cindy Reiman: Photography Manager
Karen Huang: Photo Researcher
Introduction and supplementary material by Edward Willett

Cataloging-in-Publication Data

Astronomy: understanding celestial bodies/edited by Samuel Kazlow.—First edition.
        pages cm.—(The study of science)
Audience: Grades 7–12.
Includes bibliographical references and index.
ISBN 978-1-62275-406-9 (library bound)
1. Astronomy—Juvenile literature. 2. Solar system—Juvenile literature. I. Kazlow, Samuel, editor.
QB46.A738 2015
520—dc23

2014010963

Manufactured in the United States of America

On the cover: *© iStockphoto.com/Rastan; cover and interior pages borders and backgrounds © iStockphoto.com/ LuMaxArt*

CONTENTS

INTRODUCTION

The Eagle Nebula as seen by the Infrared Space Observatory. ESA/ISO, CAM & The ISOGAL Team

Astronomy began with ancient peoples, probably even before they were fully human, looking up at the night sky and wondering at the points of light glittering across it. As human civilizations advanced, they peopled the heavens with gods and mythological creatures, imagining them looking down on the Earth below and taking a keen interest in human affairs. Those ancient stargazers looked to the skies for some hint of what the gods had planned for Earth and its people, for signs of divine pleasure or wrath.

One could say, then, that the study of the heavens has always been focused on the biggest questions of human existence: How did humans come to be here? What will happen to humans in the future? Does life exist elsewhere in the universe?

Those are still questions that astronomy attempts to answer, though scientists today are no longer trying to figure out the will of the gods by watching the movement of the stars and planets. Instead, they are trying to understand the birth and evolution of the universe.

This book examines the history of astronomy, from before the invention of the telescope through the heady advances made possible by

the advent of spectroscopes, radio telescopes, and observatories in Earth orbit, and many other technological advances.

It takes a quick tour of the universe, starting with our Earth's solar system, then moving out into Earth's galaxy, the Milky Way, where other worlds orbit other stars, and finally into intergalactic space and the billions of galaxies stretching to the unimaginably distant edge.

The book explains some of the strangest denizens of the celestial zoo, from black holes so massive that nothing can escape their gravitational pull, not even light, to quasars that can shine more brightly than entire galaxies full of stars, to the mysterious dark matter that affects the structure of the universe and yet remains an almost complete unknown.

The book concludes with the quest to answer some of the most fundamental questions science has ever faced—how the universe was born, how it has evolved, and what its ultimate fate will be—and how that quest has led to one of science's most famous theories (even lending its name to a popular television show): the *big bang theory*.

Scientists know far more about the universe and Earth's place within it than the ancient people gazing up at the star-spangled sky could have hoped to understand. Ancient peoples made up stories based on the constellations they saw in the night sky. Today, there exist actual photographs of space taken from a satellite. Modern astronomy is said to have begun in the early sixteenth century. Since then, scientists have discovered so much about the universe. Yet there is still so much more to learn. Astronomy's most exciting discoveries may well remain to be made.

CHAPTER 1

THE BASICS OF ASTRONOMY

One of the oldest of all sciences is astronomy, the study of celestial objects. That's not too surprising, since people have been looking up at the skies since before recorded history, and people who view dark skies quickly recognize that some of those points of light follow paths that are orderly and predictable.

Even though astronomy is one of the oldest sciences, new discoveries continue to flood in from modern-day astronomers. Today, of course, astronomy has moved beyond merely observing the Sun, Moon, stars, and planets from Earth's surface. Today, astronomy encompasses the study of everything outside our atmosphere—from our solar system to the stars of our galaxy to all the millions of galaxies in deep space. New technology, new theories, and new observations are leading us to ever-more-exciting insights into the astonishing complexity and diversity of our universe.

ASTRONOMY THROUGHOUT TIME

The ruins of many ancient structures indicate that their builders observed the motions of the Sun, the Moon, and other celestial bodies. The most famous of these is probably England's Stonehenge, which was built between about 3100 and 1550 BCE. Some of the monument's large stones were aligned in relationship to the position of the rising Sun on the summer solstice. Several hundreds of

The positioning of the stones in the prehistoric monument Stonehenge indicates that the site was used by ancient peoples to track the movement of the Sun and Moon. George W. Bailey/Shutterstock.com

other ancient structures showing astronomical alignment also have been found in Europe, Egypt, and the Americas.

In many early civilizations, astronomy was sufficiently advanced that reliable calendars had been developed. In ancient Egypt astronomer-priests were responsible for anticipating the season of the annual flooding of the Nile River. The Maya, who lived in what is now southeastern Mexico, Guatemala, and Belize, developed a complicated calendar system about 2,000 years ago. The Dresden Codex, a Mayan text from the 1st millennium CE, contains exceptionally accurate astronomical calculations, including tables predicting eclipses and the movements of Venus.

In China, a calendar had been developed by the 14th century BCE. In about 350 BCE a Chinese astronomer, Shih Shen, drew up what may be the earliest star catalog, listing about 800 stars. Chinese records mention comets, meteors, large sunspots, and novae.

The early Greek astronomers knew many of the geometric relationships of the heavenly bodies. A few early Greek thinkers, including Aristotle, thought Earth was a sphere. Eratosthenes, born in about 276 BCE, demonstrated its circumference. Hipparchus, who lived around 140 BCE, was a prolific and talented astronomer. Among many other accomplishments, he classified stars according to apparent brightness, estimated the size and distance of the Moon, found a way to predict eclipses, and calculated the length of the year to within 6.5 minutes.

The most influential ancient astronomer historically was Ptolemy (Claudius Ptolemaeus) of Alexandria, who lived in about 140 CE. His geometric scheme predicted the motions of the planets. In his view, Earth occupied the center of the universe. His theory approximating the true motions of the celestial bodies was held steadfastly until the end of the Middle Ages.

In medieval times Western astronomy did not progress. During those centuries Hindu and Arab astronomers kept the science alive. The records of the Arab astronomers and their translations of Greek astronomical treatises were the foundation of the later upsurge in Western astronomy.

Ptolemy believed that Earth occupied the center of the universe. Imagno/ Hulton Archive/Getty Images

Although roots can be traced back through Arab and Greek contributions, modern astronomy started with the work of Nicolaus Copernicus in Poland in the early 16th century. Copernicus concluded that the Sun, not Earth, was the center of the universe and that Earth was a planet orbiting the Sun. In 1543, the year of Copernicus's death, came the publication of his theory that Earth and the other planets revolved around the Sun. His suggestion contradicted all the authorities of the time and caused great controversy. Galileo supported Copernicus's theory with his observations that at least a few celestial bodies, namely the satellites of Jupiter, clearly did not circle Earth.

The great Danish astronomer Tycho Brahe rejected Copernicus's theory. Yet his data on planetary positions were later used to support that theory. After Tycho's death, his assistant, Johannes Kepler, analyzed Tycho's data and developed the laws of planetary motion. In 1687 Newton's law of gravitation and laws of motion explained Kepler's laws.

Meanwhile, the instruments available to astronomers were becoming more sophisticated. Beginning with Galileo, the telescope was used to reveal many hitherto invisible phenomena, such as the revolution of satellites about other planets.

In contrast to Ptolemy, Nicolaus Copernicus argued that the Sun was the center of the universe and that Earth was a planet orbiting the Sun. Fotosearch/Archive Photos/Getty Images

BEFORE THE TELESCOPE

For centuries, astronomers concentrated on learning about the motions of heavenly bodies. They saw the Sun rise in the east and set in the west. In the night sky they saw tiny points of light. Most of these lights—the stars—seemed to stay in the same place in relation to one another, as if they were all fastened to a huge black globe surrounding Earth. Other lights, however, seemed to travel, going from group to group of stationary stars. They named these moving points planets, which means "wanderers" in Greek.

When people today look at the sky without a telescope or other modern instrument, they see basically the same things the ancient astronomers saw. During the day one can see the Sun and sometimes a faint Moon. On a clear night one can see stars and usually the Moon. Sometimes a star may seem to be in different positions from night to night: it is really a planet, one of the "wanderers" of the sky. The planets all circle the Sun, just as Earth does. They are visible from Earth because sunlight bounces off them. The stars are much farther away. Most stars are like the Sun—large, hot, and bright. They shine from their own energy.

The apparent westward motion of the Sun during the day and of the stars in the night sky is actually caused by Earth's movement. Earth rotates eastward, completing one rotation each day. This may be hard to believe at first because when one thinks of motion one usually also thinks of the vibrations one feels in moving cars or trains. But Earth moves freely in space, without rubbing against anything, so it does not vibrate. It is this gentle rotation, uninhibited by significant friction, that makes the Sun and the stars appear to be rising and setting.

The development of the spectroscope in the early 1800s was a major step forward in the development of astronomical instruments. Later, photography became an invaluable aid to astronomers. They could study photographs at leisure and make microscopic measurements on them. Even more recent instrumental developments—including telescopes that detect electromagnetic radiation other than visible light, and space probes and manned spaceflights—have helped answer old questions and have opened astronomers' eyes to new problems.

HOW ASTRONOMERS STUDY THE SKIES

Astronomers are at a distinct disadvantage compared with practitioners of other sciences; with few exceptions, they cannot experiment on the objects they study. Virtually all the information available is in the form of electromagnetic radiation (such as light) arriving from distant objects. Fortunately, this radiation contains an amazing number of clues to the nature of the objects emitting it.

Electromagnetic radiation travels in the form of waves, or oscillating electric and magnetic fields. In its interaction with matter, however, it is best understood as consisting of particles, called photons. These waves occur in a vast variety of frequencies and wavelengths. In order of increasing frequency (decreasing wavelength) these parts of the electromagnetic spectrum are called radio waves, microwaves, infrared, visible light, ultraviolet, X-rays, and gamma rays. As particles, radio-wave photons carry the least amount of energy and gamma rays the most.

MAGNIFYING THE HEAVENS: TELESCOPES

Naturally, the first part of the spectrum to be studied with instruments was visible light. Telescopes, first used for astronomy by Galileo in 1609, use lenses or mirrors to form images of distant objects. These images can be viewed directly or captured using film or electronic devices. Telescopes gather more light than the naked eye and magnify the image, allowing finer details to be seen. Even though early telescopes were crude by today's standards, they almost immediately allowed discoveries such as the Moon's craters, Jupiter's moons, Saturn's rings, Venus's phases, sunspots, and thousands of previously unseen stars.

Galileo was the first to use telescopes to study astronomy. SuperStock

In the 20th century, new technologies allowed the development of telescopes capable of detecting electromagnetic radiation all the way across the spectrum. Most of the radiation emitted by many objects is at frequencies well outside the visible range. Even objects that do emit visible light often reveal much more information when studied at other wavelengths.

By the 1990s optical (visible light) telescopes reached enormous size and power, a good example being the Keck telescopes on top of Mauna Kea in Hawaii. These two telescopes have collecting mirrors 33 feet (10 meters) in diameter, allowing detection of objects millions of times fainter than can be seen with the naked eye, with detail about a thousand times finer. Actually, astronomers seldom look through such telescopes directly. Instead, they use cameras to capture images photographically or newer, more sensitive detectors to capture images electronically. Most work is now done with electronic detectors, including charge-coupled devices (CCDs).

Since the 1940s radio telescopes have made great contributions. The largest single antenna, with a dish diameter of 1,000 feet (300 meters), is the Arecibo instrument in Puerto Rico. Huge arrays of multiple telescopes, such as the Very

Large Array (VLA) in New Mexico, allow highly detailed imaging using radio waves, which otherwise yield rather "blurry" images. The largest is the Very Long Baseline Array (VLBA), consisting of 10 dishes scattered over an area more than 5,000 miles (8,000 kilometers) across. Data from these instruments are correlated using a technique called interferometry. The level of detail that can then be seen in radio-emitting objects (such as the centers of distant galaxies) is equivalent to discerning a dime at a distance of a few thousand miles.

A tremendous advance has been the placement of astronomical instruments in space. Telescopes and other instruments aboard space probes have explored all the Sun's planets at close range. At least as important, though, have been large telescopes placed in Earth orbit, above the obscuring and blurring effects of Earth's atmosphere.

The best known of these telescopes is NASA's Hubble Space Telescope, which was launched in 1990 into an orbit 380 miles (610 kilometers) above Earth's surface. It initially returned disappointing images, owing to a mistake in the grinding of its 94.5-inch (2.4-meter) primary mirror. In 1993 space shuttle astronauts installed corrective optics, and ever since it has returned magnificent data. Although Hubble is smaller than many ground-based telescopes, its view free of atmospheric distortions generally yields better images than can be obtained from the ground, leading to many discoveries. Interestingly, a technology called adaptive optics now allows many ground-based telescopes to rival Hubble's level of detail, by removing much of the blurring effect of the atmosphere.

Less well known than Hubble but perhaps just as important are several other space telescopes that specialize in other parts of the spectrum. NASA's Compton Gamma Ray Observatory (whose mission lasted from 1991 to 2000) and Chandra X-ray Observatory (launched in 1999) have sent back a flood of data about objects such as neutron stars and black holes. These objects produce high-energy radiation that is largely blocked by Earth's atmosphere. NASA's Spitzer Space Telescope (launched in 2003) detects a wide range of infrared radiation, which is emitted by cooler objects, including interstellar clouds of gas and dust, where stars and planets form.

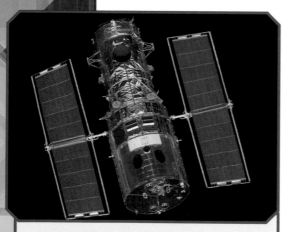

The Hubble Space Telescope appears in a photograph taken from the space shuttle Discovery *in December 1999.* NASA

THE COLORS OF SPACE:
SPECTROSCOPY

Stars give off a whole range of electromagnetic radiation. The kind of radiation emitted is related to the temperature of the star: the higher the temperature of the star, the more energy it gives off and the more this energy is concentrated in high-frequency radiation. An instrument called a spectrograph can separate radiation into the different frequencies. The array of frequencies makes up the spectrum of the star.

The color of a star is also an indication of its temperature. Red light has less energy than blue light. A reddish star must have a large amount of its energy in red light. A white or bluish star has a larger amount of higher-energy blue light, so it must be hotter than the reddish star.

Stars have bright or dark lines in their spectra. These bright or dark lines are narrow regions of extra-high emission or absorption of electromagnetic radiation. The presence of a certain chemical element, such as hydrogen or calcium, in the star causes a particular set of lines in the star's spectrum. Since most of the lines found in stellar spectra have been identified with specific chemical elements,

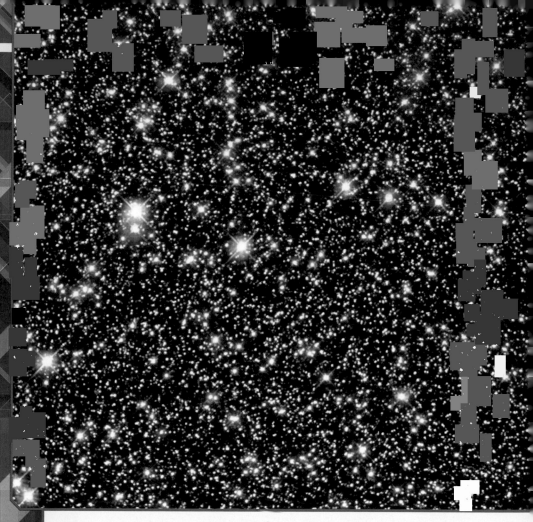

A star's color indicates its surface temperature. The stars that appear bluish or greenish in this image are hotter than the faint orange stars. The bright red stars are much cooler stars near the end of their lives. The Hubble Heritage Team (AURA/STScI/NASA)

astronomers can learn from a star's spectrum what chemical elements it contains.

Spectrum lines are useful in another way, too. When an observer sees radiation coming from a source, such as a star, the frequency of the radiation is affected by the observer's motion toward or away from the source. This is called the Doppler effect. If the observer and the star are moving away from each other, the observer detects a shift to lower frequencics. If the star and the observer are approaching each other, the shift is to higher frequencies.

Astronomers know the normal spectrum-line frequencies for many chemical elements. By comparing these known frequencies with those of the same set of lines in a star's spectrum, astronomers can tell how fast the star is moving toward or away from Earth.

SIMULATED SPACE: COMPUTER MODELS

Although astronomers mostly cannot experiment with real astronomical objects in the laboratory, they can write computer programs to employ the laws of physics to simulate the structure and behavior of the actual objects. These models are never perfect, since both computing power and detailed knowledge of the structure and composition of the objects of interest are limited. In some situations, there are even uncertainties in the laws themselves. Nonetheless, these models can be adjusted until they closely match observable features and behavior of real objects.

Among the many types of astronomical phenomena that can be modeled are the evolution of stars, planetary systems, galaxies, and even the universe itself. Models of stars have successfully simulated their observed properties and supply predictions of what happens to them as they age. Other models have shown how planets can form from rotating clouds of gas and dust. Models of the early universe allow astronomers to study how large-scale structures such as galaxies developed as gravity accentuated tiny differences in the universe's density. As computers and modeling techniques have improved, this has become an ever more important tool of astronomy.

CHAPTER 2

THE SOLAR SYSTEM

The most striking feature in Earth's sky is the Sun: giver of light and warmth, it was worshipped by many early cultures. One of the great discoveries of astronomy was the realization that Earth orbits the Sun rather than the other way around. Today we know that the Sun is orbited by a great many objects, all of which together form the solar system.

After the Sun, the major objects of the solar system are the eight planets. Other objects that form part of the solar system include dwarf planets, moons (which orbit planets or dwarf planets), asteroids, comets, meteoroids, and even microscopic particles of dust and individual atoms and molecules of various gases. The whole collection is hurtling through space at roughly 150 miles (240 kilometers) per second, as the solar system itself orbits the center of the Milky Way galaxy at a rate of about one revolution every 225 million years.

HOW IT ALL BEGAN

Astronomers believe that the solar system formed as a by-product of the formation of the Sun itself some 4.6 billion years ago. According to the prevailing theory, the Sun and its many satellites condensed out of the solar nebula, a huge interstellar cloud of gas and dust. The solar system began forming when the gravity of this interstellar cloud caused the cloud to start contracting and slowly spinning. This could have been caused by random fluctuations in the density of the cloud or by an external disturbance, such as the shock wave from an exploding star.

As the interstellar cloud squeezed inward, more and more matter became packed into the center, which became the protosun (the material that later developed into the Sun). The contraction caused the cloud to spin faster and faster and to flatten into a disk. Eventually, the center of the cloud collapsed so much that it became dense enough and hot enough for nuclear reactions to begin, and the Sun was born.

Meanwhile, away from the center the gas and dust in the spinning disk cooled. Solid grains of silicates and other minerals, the basis of rocks, condensed out of the gaseous material in the disk. Farther from the center, where temperatures were lower, ices of

Artist's conception of a young version of the solar system depicting the dusty disks thought to be the breeding grounds of planets. NASA/JPL

water, methane, ammonia, and other chemical compounds began to form. The spinning material in the disk collided and began to stick together, forming larger and larger objects. Ultimately, some of the clumped-together objects grew huge and developed into planets. The inner planets formed mostly from chunks of silicate rock and metal, while the outer planets developed mainly from ices. Smaller chunks of matter and debris that did not get incorporated into the planets became asteroids, in the inner part of the solar nebula, and comet nuclei, in the outer part of the nebula. At some point after matter in the nebula had condensed and clumped into objects, the intensity of the solar wind seems to have suddenly increased. This blew much of the rest of the gas and dust off into space.

This general formation process is thought not to be unique to the solar system but rather to be how stars and planets throughout the universe develop. Astronomers have detected disks of matter surrounding newly formed stars.

JUST ONE OF MANY

Astronomers do not know exactly how far out the solar system extends. Earth orbits the Sun at an average distance of about 93 million miles (150 million kilometers). Astronomers use this distance as a basic unit of length in describing the vast distances of the solar system. One astronomical unit (AU) is defined as the average distance between Earth and the Sun.

There are eight planets in the solar system. Neptune, the outermost planet, orbits the Sun at a distance of about 30 AU, or 2.8 billion miles (4.5 billion kilometers). Many comets have orbits that take them thousands of times farther out than Neptune. Most comets are thought to originate in the outermost parts of the solar system, the Kuiper belt and the much more distant Oort cloud. Each of these consists of countless small icy bodies that orbit the Sun. The farthest reaches of the Oort cloud extend perhaps to 100,000 AU, or some 9.3 trillion miles (15 trillion kilometers), from the Sun.

The solar system is, of course, not alone in space. The Sun is a star like countless others, and other stars also have planets circling them. The Sun is part of the Milky Way galaxy, a huge group of stars swirling around in a pinwheel shape. The galaxy contains hundreds of billions of stars. To measure the enormous distances in space, astronomers often use the light-year as a unit of length. One light-year is equal to the distance light travels in a vacuum in one year, about 5.88 trillion miles (9.46 trillion kilometers). The Milky Way galaxy is roughly 150,000 light-years across. The Sun's nearest neighbor in the galaxy is the star Proxima Centauri (part of the triple-star system named Alpha Centauri). This stellar "neighbor" lies some 4.2 light-years, or more

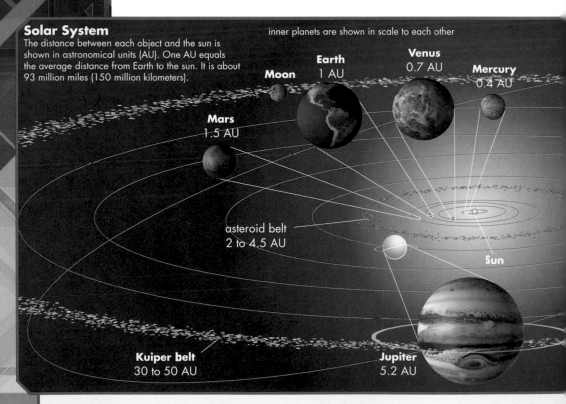

Solar System
The distance between each object and the sun is shown in astronomical units (AU). One AU equals the average distance from Earth to the sun. It is about 93 million miles (150 million kilometers).

inner planets are shown in scale to each other

Moon

Earth
1 AU

Venus
0.7 AU

Mercury
0.4 AU

Mars
1.5 AU

asteroid belt
2 to 4.5 AU

Sun

Kuiper belt
30 to 50 AU

Jupiter
5.2 AU

The solar system consists of the planets that orbit the Sun as well as such smaller bodies as dwarf planets, comets, and asteroids. Encyclopædia Britannica, Inc.

than 25 trillion miles (40 trillion kilometers), away from the Sun.

Outside the Milky Way galaxy there are billions more galaxies stretching out through space. Astronomers cannot see to the end of the universe, but they have detected galaxies and other objects that are several billion light-years away from the Sun. Compared with such distances, the space that the solar system occupies seems tiny.

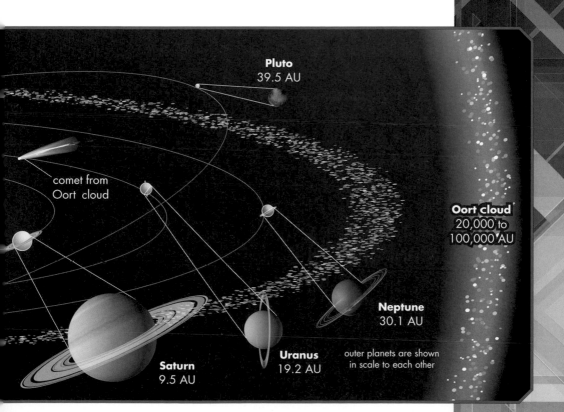

Pluto
39.5 AU

comet from
Oort cloud

Oort cloud
20,000 to
100,000 AU

Neptune
30.1 AU

Uranus
19.2 AU

outer planets are shown
in scale to each other

Saturn
9.5 AU

ANATOMY OF THE SOLAR SYSTEM

The Sun is the central and dominant member of the solar system. Its gravitational force holds the other members in orbit and governs their motions. The largest members of the solar system after the Sun are the planets and the dwarf planets and their moons. The other natural bodies in the solar system are called small bodies. They include asteroids, meteoroids, comets, and the billions of icy objects in the Kuiper belt and Oort cloud.

The small bodies and the smaller moons can be quite irregularly shaped. The planets, the dwarf planets, and the larger moons are nearly spherical in shape. They are large enough so that their own gravity squeezes them into the general shape of a ball. The shapes of the planets and dwarf planets that rotate especially rapidly are distorted to various degrees. Instead of being perfect spheres, such bodies have some flattening at the poles, which makes them appear squashed.

Most objects in the solar system have elliptical, or oval-shaped, orbits around the Sun. These objects include the planets, dwarf planets, asteroids, comets, and Kuiper-belt objects. The planets orbit the Sun in nearly circular orbits, while the small bodies tend to have much more eccentric, or elongated, orbits. The orbits of the planets lie in very nearly the same plane as the Sun's equator. The small bodies again differ, generally orbiting in planes that are more inclined, or tilted, relative to the plane of the Sun's equator. Comets whose orbits take them very far from the Sun tend to have especially eccentric and inclined orbits.

Many of those comets also orbit in a different direction than most other objects in the solar system. The Sun rotates in a counterclockwise direction as viewed from a vantage point above Earth's North Pole. The planets, dwarf planets, asteroids, and Kuiper-belt objects and many comets orbit the Sun in the same direction that the Sun rotates. This is called prograde, or direct, motion. The comets with large orbits and the icy bodies of the Oort cloud are thought to be distributed randomly in all directions of the sky. Many of these objects orbit the Sun in retrograde motion, or the direction opposite to that of the Sun's rotation.

OUR STAR

The Sun far outweighs all other components of the solar system combined. In fact, the Sun contains more than 99 percent of the mass of the entire solar system. Nevertheless, the Sun is a fairly average-sized star. From Earth it looks so much larger and brighter than other stars only because it is so much nearer to Earth than any other star. If the Sun were much farther away, it would look pretty much like many other stars in the night sky. But if this were so, life as we know it could not exist on Earth. The Sun provides nearly all the heat, light, and other forms of energy necessary for life on Earth. In fact, the Sun provides the great majority of the energy of the solar system.

THE PLANETS AND THEIR DWARF SIBLINGS

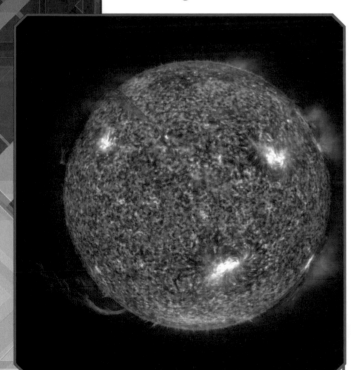

The Sun as imaged in extreme ultraviolet light by the Earth-orbiting Solar and Heliospheric Observatory (SOHO) satellite. Nearly white areas are the hottest; deeper reds indicate cooler temperatures. NASA

The most massive members

of the solar system after the Sun are the planets. Even so, their combined mass is less than 0.2 percent of the total mass of the solar system, and Jupiter accounts for a very large share of that percentage. From nearest to farthest from the Sun, the eight planets are Mercury, Venus, Earth, Mars, Jupiter, Saturn, Uranus, and Neptune.

Pluto had been considered the solar system's ninth planet from the time of its discovery in 1930 until 2006, when the International Astronomical Union (the organization that approves the names of astronomical objects for the scientific community) changed its designation. The organization created a new category of object called dwarf planet and made Pluto, Eris, and Ceres the first members of the group. Pluto and Eris are also considered Kuiper-belt objects, and Ceres is also the largest asteroid. As their name suggests, dwarf planets are similar to the eight major planets but are smaller.

The eight planets can be divided into two groups, the inner planets and the outer planets, according to their nearness to the Sun and their physical properties. The four inner planets—Mercury, Venus, Earth, and Mars—are composed mostly of silicate rock and iron and other metals in varying proportions. They all have solid surfaces and are more than three

times as dense as water. These rocky planets are also known as the terrestrial, or Earth-like, planets.

In sharp contrast, the four outer planets—Jupiter, Saturn, Uranus, and Neptune—have no solid surfaces. Jupiter and Saturn consist mainly of liquid and gaseous hydrogen and helium; Uranus and Neptune have melted ices as well as hydrogen and helium. All the outer planets are less than twice as dense as water. In fact, Saturn's density is so low that it would float if put in water. The outer planets are also much larger than the inner planets, and they have deep gaseous atmospheres. Because of this, these planets are sometimes nicknamed the gas giants. Since Jupiter is the outstanding representative of this group, the four outer planets are also known as the Jovian, or Jupiter-like, planets.

The eight planets are not distributed evenly in space. The four inner planets are much closer to each other than the four outer planets are to one another.

RINGS AND MOONS

Six of the eight planets have smaller bodies—their natural satellites, or moons—circling them. All the outer planets have numerous moons: Jupiter and Saturn have more than 60 known moons each, Uranus has more than 25, and Neptune has more than 10. The inner planets have few or none: Mars has two moons, Earth has only one, and Venus and Mercury lack moons. Many asteroids and Kuiper-belt objects, including the dwarf planets Pluto, Eris, and Haumea, also have moons.

The largest natural satellite in the solar system is Jupiter's moon Ganymede. Next in size are Saturn's moon Titan, Jupiter's Callisto and Io, Earth's Moon, and Jupiter's Europa. Both Ganymede and Titan are larger than the planet Mercury. Earth's Moon is so large with respect to Earth that the two bodies have sometimes been considered a double-planet system. The solar system's smallest moons, most of which orbit Jupiter and Saturn, are less than 5 miles (8 kilometers) in diameter.

Most of the solar system's larger moons, including Earth's, orbit their planet in the same direction in which the planets orbit the Sun. A notable exception is Triton, which is Neptune's largest moon. It orbits in retrograde motion, as do many of the small, outer moons of the gas giants. Most of the solar system's moons also orbit their planet in the plane of the planet's equator. Again, Triton and many of the small, outer moons of the outer planets are exceptions, having highly inclined orbits. Moons that orbit in retrograde motion or that have inclined orbits or both are called irregular moons.

Saturn's spectacular rings are well known, but all the other outer planets also have

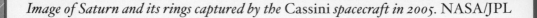

Image of Saturn and its rings captured by the Cassini *spacecraft in 2005.* NASA/JPL

systems of thin, flat rings. Each of the rings is composed of countless small pieces of matter orbiting the planet like tiny satellites. None of the inner planets has rings.

OUR MOON

The most prominent feature in the night sky is Earth's satellite, the Moon. Because of its nearness to Earth, the Moon is second only to the Sun in apparent brightness among celestial objects. It also appears roughly the same size as the Sun, though the Sun is actually about 400 times larger and 400 times more distant. In astronomical terms, however, the Moon is a fairly ordinary rocky object. Its light is simply reflected sunlight, with dim reflected light from Earth sometimes visible on the part not lit by the Sun.

The Moon is rather large in comparison to its primary planet, being over a quarter the diameter of Earth. Only the dwarf planet Pluto's satellite Charon has a larger relative size—over half the diameter of Pluto itself. The Moon's relatively large size gives it a significant influence on Earth, most evident in the ocean tides, which are a result of the Moon's gravitational pull on Earth and its oceans.

The Moon does not always look the same from Earth. Sometimes it looks round, sometimes like a thin, curved sliver. These apparent changes are called the phases of the Moon. They occur because the Moon shines only when the Sun's light bounces off its surface. This means that only the side of the Moon that faces the Sun is bright.

The angle between the Sun and the Moon in the sky determines what fraction of the side of the Moon facing Earth is lit, giving rise to the succession of phases. The phase cycle is often considered to start with the "new" Moon, which is invisible from Earth. In this phase the Moon is directly or almost directly between Earth and the Sun, so the entire sunlit portion of the Moon faces away from Earth. The Moon's orbit carries it eastward relative to the Sun in the sky, so that a few days after new, the Moon appears in the early evening as a crescent, with the lit side facing west, toward where the Sun has just set. The rest of the Moon's disk may be faintly visible from light reflected off Earth. This crescent Moon sets a few hours after the Sun.

About a week after new, the Moon appears half lit and high in the sky, 90 degrees east of the Sun, at sunset. This Moon, called first quarter (being a quarter of the way through its monthly cycle), will have risen at about noon and may have been visible in a blue sky during the afternoon. For the next few nights, the Moon comes up later in the afternoon and continues to wax, or show a greater illuminated fraction. During this time it is referred to as gibbous, or between half and full. About two weeks after new, it rises as a full Moon more or less in the east—opposite the Sun—at sunset. The full Moon stays up all night, setting more or less in the west at about sunrise.

After its full phase, the Moon rises later and later each evening, passing through waning (progressively less illuminated) gibbous phases. Then, at third quarter, it appears as a "half" Moon with its eastern half lit. In this phase, the Moon rises at about midnight, is highest at sunrise, and sets at about noon. Finally, after a few days of waning crescents, the Moon returns to new, 29.53 days after the last new Moon. Actually, the Moon orbits Earth with a period of 27.32 days, but during this time Earth will have moved almost 1/12 of the way around the Sun, so 2.21 extra days are needed for the Moon to get back to its position between Earth and the Sun.

HOW ECLIPSES HAPPEN

The Moon's path through the sky, as seen against the background of stars, is very close to the Sun's path, called the ecliptic. For this reason, it is possible at new Moon for the Moon to pass directly between Earth and the Sun, casting its shadow on Earth. During such an event—called a solar eclipse—the Moon partially or totally blocks the Sun's light. If the Moon is a bit closer to Earth than on average, it appears large enough in the sky to completely cover the Sun's disk for up to about 7 minutes. Such total eclipses are spectacular events, with the Sun's corona, or outer atmosphere, visible around the black disk of the Moon in a daytime sky nearly as dark as night. The path of total eclipse is typically only about 100 miles (160 kilometers) wide. Observers in the area around the path of totality see only part of the Sun blocked, and people outside that area do not see an eclipse.

It is also possible for Earth to be exactly between the Sun and the Moon, thereby casting a shadow on the Moon. This is called a lunar eclipse, and it naturally happens at full Moon. If the Moon passes completely into Earth's shadow, the eclipse is called total and the previously full Moon almost completely disappears from the night sky. Only dim reddish sunlight refracted onto the Moon by Earth's atmosphere renders it visible.

If the Moon's and Sun's apparent paths in the sky were identical, lunar and solar eclipses would happen every month. However, the Moon's orbit is inclined about 5 degrees relative to Earth's orbit around the Sun, so that the alignment is usually not good enough for either type of eclipse to occur. Both types of eclipse can be predicted with great precision.

ASTEROIDS: BIG CHUNKS

Numerous rocky small bodies are called aster-oids, or minor planets. Their orbits lie, for the most part, in a doughnut-shaped zone between the orbits of Mars and Jupiter. This zone is known as the main asteroid belt. The asteroids are not distributed evenly in the main belt. Rather there are several gaps in their orbits, owing to the influence of Jupiter's gravitational force. The asteroids outside the main belt include the near-Earth asteroids, which come within at least about 28 million miles (45 million kilometers) of Earth's orbit. The orbits of some of these asteroids even cross Earth's orbit.

Ceres is the largest asteroid, with a diam-eter of roughly 585 miles (940 kilometers). The asteroids Pallas and Vesta each have a diameter greater than 300 miles (485 kilometers). Few asteroids, however, are larger than 100 miles (160 kilometers) across, and the numbers of asteroids increase dramatically at smaller sizes. It is estimated that millions of asteroids of boulder size exist in the solar system.

Astronomers think that the asteroids are chunks of material left over from the process that created the inner planets. The huge pull of Jupiter's gravity prevented these rocky chunks

from clumping together into a large planet. Many of the smaller asteroids are thought to be fragments caused by collisions between the larger asteroids. Some of these fragments collide with Earth as meteorites.

The three main types of asteroids seem to be rich in organic compounds, stony materials, and iron and other metals, respectively. Some asteroids are thought to contain samples of the first materials to coalesce out of the great cloud of gas and dust from which the solar system itself is believed to have formed.

METEOROIDS: SMALL CHUNKS

Meteoroids are small chunks of rock, metal, or other material in interplanetary space. The vast majority of meteoroids are small fragments of asteroids. Other meteoroids are fragments from the Moon or Mars, while some may be rocky debris shed by comets.

When a meteoroid collides with Earth's atmosphere, it is usually vaporized by heat from friction with the air molecules. The bright streak of light that occurs while the particle vaporizes is called a meteor. Occasionally, a large chunk of rock and metal survives the journey through the atmosphere, reaching the ground. Such remnants are called meteorites.

Meteorites have also been identified on Mars, and pieces of meteorites were found in rock samples collected by astronauts on the Moon.

COMETS: ICY BITS

At times, a fuzzy spot of light, perhaps with a tail streaming away from it, appears in the sky. Such appearances of the small icy bodies called comets are spectacular but infrequent. Comets are only easily visible from Earth when they pass close to the Sun. Most comets that are detected from Earth are visible only with a telescope. Occasionally, one can be seen with the unaided eye, and several times a century a comet will appear that can be seen even in the daytime.

Just as the asteroids are the rocky remnants of the process that formed the inner planets, the comets are thought to be leftover icy material from the formation of the outermost planets, Uranus and Neptune. Comets contain particles of rock dust and organic compounds, water ice, and ices of various substances that are normally gases on Earth. As a comet approaches the Sun, the ices turn to vapor, forming a hazy, gaseous atmosphere, or coma, around a core of solid particles, the nucleus. As the comet moves even closer to

Comet Hyakutake approached Earth to within about 9 million miles (14 million kilometers) in the spring of 1996, appearing from Earth as one of the brightest comets of the 20th century. NASA

the Sun, even more material is vaporized. Radiation and high-energy particles streaming out from the Sun may push material away from the comet into one or more long, glowing tails, which point generally away from the Sun. A comet may disintegrate completely, ending up as a swarm of tiny particles, or continue along its orbital path. As a comet moves away from the Sun, it loses its coma and tail. The only permanent part of the comet is its solid nucleus. Eventually, it may end up as a dormant, or dead, comet, after all its ices have vaporized from near its surface. Dormant comets resemble asteroids.

A comet may exist as a nucleus for thousands of years or more in the cold outer reaches of the solar system before its orbit takes it near the Sun again. The billions of distant icy objects in the Kuiper belt and the Oort cloud are, in fact, comet nuclei. These objects are thought to have orbited as nuclei for eons, without ever having approached the Sun. Sometimes the orbit of one of the objects in the Kuiper belt or the Oort cloud is disturbed by the gravity of another body so that the object is sent on a path that takes it closer to the Sun. This process is thought to be the source of most comets. For instance, one way the orbits of Oort-cloud objects might be altered is by the gravity of passing stars.

The Kuiper belt and the Oort cloud, then, can be considered vast reservoirs of comets. The Kuiper belt is a doughnut-shaped zone of several millions of comet nuclei. They orbit the Sun beyond the orbit of Neptune, mainly between about 30 and 50 AU from the Sun. The region for the most part lies fairly close to the plane of the Sun's equator (the plane in which the planets orbit). Some Kuiper-belt objects have almost circular orbits that fall near this plane. Others have very elongated, highly inclined orbits. Among the latter group are Eris and Pluto, the largest known members of the Kuiper belt.

The Kuiper belt is thought to be the source of most of the short-period comets, or those that complete an orbit around the Sun in fewer than 200 years, and especially those that take fewer than 20 years to circle the Sun once. The comet nuclei called Centaur objects are also believed to have originated in the Kuiper belt. This group of icy objects is found mainly between the orbits of the outer planets, or about 5 to 30 AU from the Sun.

Most of the long-period comets, those that take more than 200 years to orbit the Sun, are thought to come from the Oort cloud. Most of these comets have very long orbital periods, with some taking many millions of years to circle the Sun once. The Oort cloud lies much farther from the Sun than the Kuiper belt does, extending from perhaps 20,000 to 100,000 AU from the Sun. It is not a flat ring but a roughly spherical shell of probably many billions of icy small bodies orbiting in all directions.

In the middle of the 20th century, astronomers first postulated that the Kuiper belt and the Oort cloud must exist. However, because of their great distance from Earth, Kuiper-belt objects were not directly detected until the 1990s, when light detectors that were sufficiently sensitive became available. The first object in the belt to be detected was discovered in 1992, and many more large objects have since been found. (Astronomers did not begin to consider Pluto a Kuiper-belt object until several other similar objects were found in the belt.) However, none of the much more distant small bodies in the Oort cloud has been seen directly.

INTERPLANETARY MEDIUM: THE TINY STUFF

In the spaces between the planets and other bodies lie vast stretches of extremely thinly distributed matter called the interplanetary medium. The matter includes tiny particles called interplanetary dust,

or micrometeorites, along with electrically charged particles, tiny amounts of hydrogen gas, and cosmic rays.

The relatively small amounts of interplanetary dust appear to be orbiting the Sun in a disk that extends throughout the solar system in or near the plane of the planets' orbits. On a clear night a faint glow is visible in the sky along the line of the zodiac, following the setting Sun or preceding the rising Sun. This glow can be almost as bright as the Milky Way. It is caused by sunlight reflected by the interplanetary dust. Astronomers estimate that about 30,000 tons (27,000 metric tons) of the dust enter Earth's upper atmosphere each year. Spacecraft have detected such dust particles in space nearly as far as the orbit of Uranus. Most of the interplanetary dust is thought to come from the collisions of asteroids and from comets, which lose matter when they approach the Sun.

The Sun itself contributes much material to the vast spaces between the planets and other bodies. Along with the radiation that continuously leaves its surface, the Sun gives off a stream of electrically charged particles—mostly electrons and protons (plasma). This flow of particles is the solar wind. The solar wind spreads beyond the planets to the heliopause, which is the boundary between the interplanetary medium and the interstellar medium, the diffuse matter between the stars. The part of the solar wind that encounters Earth causes the auroras, or the northern and southern lights. The solar wind causes auroras on other planets, too.

The interplanetary medium also includes cosmic rays, which are high-speed, high-energy particles (atomic nuclei and electrons). Some of the cosmic rays come from the Sun, but most originate outside the solar system.

A luminous loop of the southern lights appears above Earth. Such auroras are caused by electrically charged particles of the solar wind colliding with gases in Earth's atmosphere. NASA/Johnson Space Center/Earth Sciences and Image Analysis Laboratory

THE FATE OF THE SOLAR SYSTEM

The future of the solar system probably depends on the behavior of the Sun. If current theories of stellar evolution are correct, the Sun will have much the same size and temperature for about 5 billion more years. By then, all of the hydrogen in its core will have been used up. Other nuclear reactions will begin in a shell around the core. Then the Sun will grow much brighter and larger, turning into a red giant and expanding beyond the orbit of Venus, perhaps even engulfing Earth. Much later, when all its nuclear energy sources are exhausted, the Sun will cool down, evolving into a white dwarf star. Around it will orbit the remaining planets. They will have turned into frozen chunks, orbiting their shrunken star.

CHAPTER 3

THE STARS

B esides the Sun, Moon and planets, the other striking feature of the night sky is the stars: countless numbers of small lights that swing across the sky every night but remain fixed relative to each other. Some of the brighter stars seem to form patterns, with different cultures interpreting those patterns—known as constellations—in various ways, as animals, people, or objects. Once you recognize a few basic constellations—Orion and Scorpius are among the easiest to identify—you can use them as signposts to help you find other constellations and stars.

HOW DO WE LOCATE THEM?

Astronomers need to record the exact locations of stars. Within limits, it is useful to locate objects within constellations. Numerical coordinate systems are used to record the locations of celestial objects more

New stars are forming from the hot gas and dust of the Orion Nebula, a type of nebula known as an H II region. More than 500 separate images were combined to create this mosaic. NASA, ESA, M. Robberto (Space Telescope Science Institute/ESA) and the Hubble Space Telescope Orion Treasury Project Team precisely. These systems are like the coordinate system of latitude and longitude used for Earth.

Different celestial coordinate systems have been devised. To be useful they must take into account that Earth has two regular motions in relation to the stars. Its rotation causes the sphere of stars to appear to make a complete circle around the planet once a day. And Earth's revolution around the Sun causes the apparent star positions at a particular hour to shift from day to day, so that they return to their "original" position after a year.

The horizon, or azimuth, system is based on the north-south circle that passes through the observer's zenith (the highest point in the sky) and the observer's horizon. It uses two angles called azimuth and altitude. Azimuth locates the star relative to the north-south line, and altitude locates it relative to the plane of the horizon. For this system to be useful, the time of the observation and the location from which the observation was made must be accurately known.

The equator system is based on the concept of the celestial sphere. All the stars and other heavenly bodies can be imagined to be located on a huge sphere that surrounds Earth. The sphere has several imaginary lines and points. One such line is the celestial equator, which is the projection of Earth's equator onto the celestial sphere. Another is the line of the ecliptic, which is the Sun's apparent yearly path along this sphere. The celestial equator and the ecliptic intersect at two points, called the vernal equinox and the autumnal equinox. (When the Sun is at either point, day and night on Earth are equally long.) The north and south celestial poles are extensions of the North and South poles of Earth along Earth's axis of rotation.

In the equator system the position of a star is given by coordinates called declination and right ascension. The declination locates the star by its angular distance north or south of the celestial equator. The right ascension locates the star by its angular distance east or west of the vernal equinox. Since this system is attached to the celestial sphere, all points on Earth (except the poles) are continually changing their positions under the coordinate system.

HOW FAR AWAY ARE THEY?

Fixing stars on an imaginary sphere is useful for finding them from Earth, but it does not reveal their actual locations. One way to measure the distances of nearby stars from Earth is the parallax method.

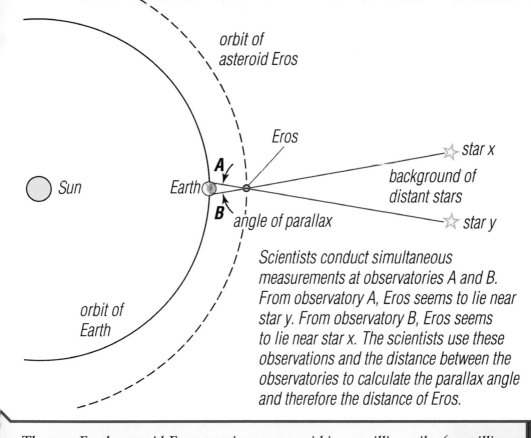

orbit of
asteroid Eros

Eros

Sun

Earth

A

B

angle of parallax

star x

background of
distant stars

star y

orbit of
Earth

Scientists conduct simultaneous
measurements at observatories A and B.
From observatory A, Eros seems to lie near
star y. From observatory B, Eros seems
to lie near star x. The scientists use these
observations and the distance between the
observatories to calculate the parallax angle
and therefore the distance of Eros.

The near-Earth asteroid Eros sometimes comes within 14 million miles (22 million kilometers) of Earth. At such a near approach, its distance is easy to measure using the parallax method. Encyclopædia Britannica, Inc.

For parallax measurements of stars, scientists make use of Earth's yearly motion around the Sun. Because of this motion, observers on Earth view the stars from different positions at different times of the year. At any given time of year, Earth is 186 million miles (300 million kilometers) away on the opposite side of the Sun from where it was six months before. Two photographs of a near star taken through a large telescope six months apart will show that the star appears to shift against the background of more distant stars. If this shift is large enough to be measured, astronomers can calculate the distance to the star.

More than four centuries ago the phenomenon of parallax was used to counter Nicolaus Copernicus's suggestion that Earth travels around the Sun. Scientists of the time pointed out that if it did, stars should show an annual change in direction due to parallax. But, using the instruments available to them, they were unable to measure any parallax, so they concluded that Copernicus was wrong. Astronomers now know that the stars are all at such tremendous distances from Earth that their parallax angles are extremely difficult to measure. Even modern instruments cannot measure the parallax of most stars.

Astronomers measure parallaxes of stars in seconds of arc. This is a tiny unit of measure; for example, a penny must be 2.5 miles (4 kilometers) away before it appears as small as one second of arc. Yet no star except the Sun is close enough to have a parallax that large. Alpha Centauri, a member of the group of three stars nearest to the Sun, has a parallax of about three quarters of a second of arc.

Astronomers have devised a unit of distance called the parsec—the distance at which the angle opposite the base of a triangle measures one second of arc when the base of the triangle is the radius of Earth's orbit around the Sun. One parsec is equal to 19.2 trillion miles (30.9 trillion kilometers). Alpha Centauri is about 1.3 parsecs distant.

Another unit used to record large astronomical distances is the light-year. This is the distance that light travels within a vacuum in one year—about 5.88 trillion miles (9.46 trillion kilometers), or about 0.31 parsec. Proxima Centauri, part of the Alpha Centauri system, is the star closest to Earth (apart from the Sun), yet it is about 4.2 light-years distant. Light takes more than four years to reach Earth from that distance.

Since parallax yields distances to only relatively nearby stars, other methods must be used for more distant ones. One of these methods is statistical parallax, in which the apparent motions across the sky of groups of stars are analyzed to determine their probable distance. Another method involves observing certain stars that vary regularly in brightness.

HOW BIG AND BRIGHT ARE THEY?

Both the size and the temperature of a star determine how much radiation energy it gives off each second: this is the actual brightness of the star. It is also true, however, that the closer a star is to Earth, the more of its radiation energy will actually reach Earth and the brighter it will appear.

The brightest stars in this field are yellow stars similar to the Sun; smaller, dim stars are red dwarfs. Photo AURA/STScI/NASA/ JPL (NASA photo # STScI-PRC95-32)

Astronomers express the brightness of a star in terms of its magnitude. Two values of magnitude describe a star. The apparent magnitude refers to how bright the star looks from Earth. The absolute magnitude of a star is the value its apparent magnitude would have if the star were 10 parsecs from Earth. The apparent magnitude of a star depends on not only its distance but also its temperature and size. The temperature is found from its spectrum; if the distance is known, then astronomers can calculate the size of the star and also assign a value for its absolute magnitude. The actual brightness of stars may be compared using their absolute magnitudes.

Certain stars whose brightness varies regularly provide an important way for astronomers to estimate the distances of remote galaxies. In such stars the actual brightness (absolute magnitude) is closely related to the period of their brightness variations. Astronomers can use the observed period to determine the actual brightness and then compare this with the apparent brightness to estimate the distance.

Astronomers have discovered all kinds of stars—from huge, brilliant red supergiants more than 100 times the Sun's diameter to extremely dense neutron stars only about 12 miles (19 kilometers) across. The Sun lies in about the middle range of size and brightness of stars. The largest stars are the cool, reddish supergiants: they have low surface temperatures, but they are so bright that they must be extremely large to give off that much energy. White dwarf stars, on the other hand, are very faint in spite of their high surface

temperatures and thus must be very small—only about the size of Earth.

WHAT ARE THEY?

Astronomers have found, using analyses of stars' spectra, that stars are made mostly of the simplest elements: hydrogen and helium. These elements are in the gaseous state. In most of the star, however, the temperature is so high (thousands to millions of degrees) that the gas is ionized (with electrons stripped away from the atomic nuclei)—a state called plasma.

The mutual gravitational attraction of a star's matter is what forces it into a roughly spherical shape. In fact, if there were nothing to counteract this inward force, the star would collapse to a very small size. The gravitational squeezing of the gas, however, heats it to very high temperatures. In the 1800s astronomers believed that this compression was actually the energy source for a star. This presented a problem. The Sun could shine like this for only a few million years without shrinking so much that conditions on Earth would be greatly altered. Yet geological and biological evidence suggested that Earth has maintained the conditions for life for hundreds of millions of years.

Following the discovery of nuclear energy in the 20th century, astronomers were able to explain the Sun's long-lasting power output as the result of nuclear fusion: hydrogen deep inside the Sun was being fused together to form helium. This process is so energetic that it can counterbalance the inward force of gravity. Stars, then, are essentially battlegrounds between two forces—the inward crush of gravity and the outward pressure from the heat generated by nuclear fusion.

THE LIFE CYCLE OF A STAR

Stars are believed to form when large clouds of gas and dust, called nebulae, contract gravitationally (though other forces may also play a role). Eventually they become hot enough (several million degrees) in the center to start fusion of hydrogen into helium. By this time, the gas is glowing brightly, and a star is born.

This cannot last forever, though, as eventually most of the hydrogen "fuel" is converted into helium. In the largest stars, this takes only a few million years. Very-low-mass stars, with less gravitational pressure to battle, consume their fuel very slowly and may last a trillion years. The Sun

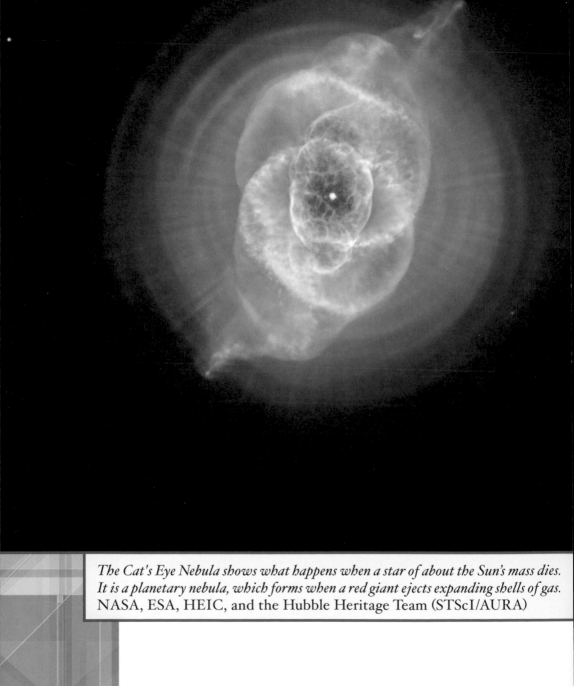

The Cat's Eye Nebula shows what happens when a star of about the Sun's mass dies. It is a planetary nebula, which forms when a red giant ejects expanding shells of gas. NASA, ESA, HEIC, and the Hubble Heritage Team (STScI/AURA)

is intermediate, with an estimated lifetime of about 10 billion years, with the Sun currently about halfway through its lifetime.

When a star's core has been converted mainly into helium, dramatic changes occur in its structure. Computer models, backed up by observations of many stars at different stages, predict that stars like the Sun will swell to about a hundred times their former diameter. After a relatively short period as such a red giant, the star will lose its outer layers, leaving a small, hot core. The core will then shrink to form a white dwarf star. Hundreds of such objects have been observed, generally confirming the predictions.

Stars born with much more mass than the Sun undergo even more dramatic events. Under tremendous pressure, such a star performs numerous additional fusion reactions in its core, producing a wide range of chemical elements, from light elements up to and including iron. At this point, the ultradense core can collapse suddenly, leading to a colossal explosion called a supernova. Many such events have been observed from Earth, some so bright that they were visible in broad daylight. For a few weeks the exploding star can outshine an entire galaxy of a hundred billion stars. The elements thrown out into space can become part of nebulae, eventually to be incorporated into future generations of stars and planets.

DENSE MATTER: NEUTRON STARS AND BLACK HOLES

After some types of supernova explosions, an extremely dense core remains. This object, called a neutron star, is about the mass of the Sun and is made mostly of neutrons. Its matter is so compact that a teaspoon of it has the mass of a small mountain. Some neutron stars spin rapidly while beaming radiation into space. If a beam intercepts Earth, astronomers may detect it as a series of pulses of radio waves or sometimes radiation at other wavelengths. Such a neutron star is referred to as a pulsar.

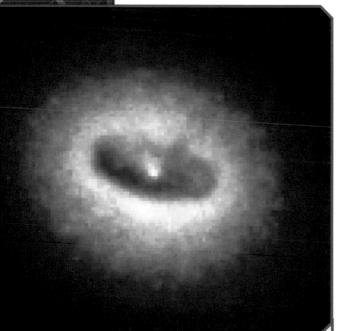

A picture from the Hubble Space Telescope shows a huge ring of gas and dust in space. Scientists think the ring may surround a black hole. Walter Jaffe/ Leiden Observatory, Holland Ford/JHU/ STScI, and NASA

BLACK HOLES: THE STRANGEST OF ALL

Black holes seem more like science fiction than reality. But since 1916, when Albert Einstein developed his general theory of relativity, scientists have known that black holes may exist, and in 1994 astronomers confirmed the existence of a black hole.

Einstein's theory suggested that if gravity could become strong enough, it would rob light of all its energy, trapping it in the same way in which it traps a planet's atmosphere. For gravity to be that strong, however, its source would have to be an extremely dense object, one with a very large mass compressed into a very small space. In 1916 the German astronomer Karl Schwarzschild calculated just how compressed a star would have to be for its gravity to trap light. According to Schwarzschild's calculations, a star the size of the Sun—864,950 miles (1,392,000 kilometers) in diameter—would have to shrink to less than 1.9 miles (3 kilometers) wide.

Even more massive stars may collapse to such high densities that their powerful gravitational pull will not allow even light, or anything else, to escape. They are called black holes. Black holes resulting from the collapse of a single, dying star may be less than 30 miles (48 kilometers), but much larger ones—with the mass of millions of suns and the size of

the solar system—are suspected to exist in the centers of many galaxies.

Often, neutron stars and black holes are detectable only because of their effects on nearby companion stars. Gas (mainly hydrogen) is drawn off the companion star and then swirls rapidly down onto (or into) the neutron star or black hole. The violent compressional heating and acceleration of the gas causes it to emit X-rays, which can be detected from Earth-based satellites. Such double star systems are called X-ray binaries.

PLANETS ORBITING OTHER STARS

Astronomers have long thought that, like the Sun, many or most stars should be accompanied by orbiting planets. These planets would be so distant from Earth, however, that their very faint light would be drowned out by the bright light of their "suns." It turns out that there are indirect methods of detecting such planets. An orbiting planet would cause a star to wobble slightly, and this wobble could be detected as alternating red and blue Doppler shifts of the star's light. Furthermore, the speed and period of the wobble could enable astronomers to estimate the planet's mass and distance from the star. This technique was first successfully used in 1995 to find a planet orbiting the star 51 Pegasi. During the next 10 years, about 140 extrasolar planets were discovered in this way (plus a few by other means, such as the dip in light caused when a planet passes in front of a star). In 2012 astronomers identified a very slight wobbling of one of the stars of Alpha Centauri, discovering a rocky, roughly Earth-sized planet orbiting the star at an extremely close distance. It is the nearest extrasolar planet to Earth.

Most of the planets found so far are at least as massive as Jupiter, yet they are closer to their stars than Mercury is to the Sun. Such close-in, massive planets should be the easiest to detect, since they cause the greatest wobbles. But they are still a challenge to explain. Current theories of planet formation suggest that such large planets should form farther from the star, where temperatures are cold enough to allow collection of large amounts of gas. One possibility astronomers are considering is that these "hot Jupiters" formed farther out from their stars and migrated inward. This raises the question, though, of why our solar system has not experienced such planetary migration.

BETWEEN THE STARS

The space between the stars contains gas and dust at extremely low densities. This matter tends to clump into clouds. These clouds are called nebulae when they block more distant starlight, reflect starlight, or get heated by stars so that they glow. Interstellar dust is made of fine particles or grains. Although only a few of these grains are spread through 1 cubic mile (4 cubic kilometers) of space, the distances between the stars are so great that the dust can block the light from distant stars. Many small, dark regions are known where few or no stars can be seen. These are dark nebulae, dust clouds of higher than average density that are thick enough to obscure the light beyond them.

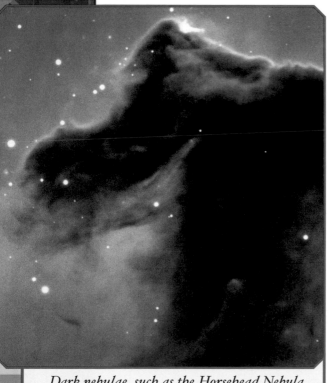

Dark nebulae, such as the Horsehead Nebula in Orion, consist of clouds of interstellar dust, which scatter starlight. VLT/ESO

Dust grains block blue light more than red light, so the color of a star can appear different if it is seen through much dust. To find the temperature of such a star, astronomers must estimate its color to be bluer than it appears because so much of its blue light is lost in the dust. When clouds of dust occur near bright stars they often reflect the starlight in all directions. Such clouds are known as reflection nebulae.

Interstellar gas is about 100 times denser than the dust but still has an extremely low density. The gas does not interfere with starlight passing through it, so it is usually difficult to detect. When a gas cloud occurs close to a hot star, however, the star's radiation causes the gas to glow. This forms a type of bright nebula known as an H II region. Away from hot stars interstellar gas is quite cool. Masses of this cool gas are called H I regions.

Interstellar gas, like most stars, consists mainly of the lightest element, hydrogen, with small amounts of helium and only traces of the other elements. The hydrogen readily glows in the hot H II regions. In the cool H I regions the hydrogen gives off radio-frequency radiation. Most interstellar gas can be located only by detecting these radio waves.

The hydrogen occurs partly as single atoms and partly as molecules (two hydrogen atoms joined together). Molecular hydrogen is even more difficult to detect than atomic hydrogen, but it must exist in abundance. Other molecules have been found in the interstellar gas because they give off low-frequency radiation. These molecules contain other atoms besides hydrogen: oxygen or carbon occurs in hydroxyl radicals (OH-) and in carbon monoxide (CO), formaldehyde (HCHO), and many others, including many organic molecules.

Wherever there are large numbers of young stars, there are also large quantities of interstellar gas and dust. New stars are constantly being formed out of the gas and dust in regions where the clouds have high densities. Although many stars blow off part of their material back into the interstellar regions, the gas and dust are slowly being used up. Astronomers theorize that eventually a time will be reached when no new stars can be formed, and star systems will slowly fade as the stars burn out one by one.

CHAPTER 4

THE GALAXIES

S tars do not usually exist all alone in space. Instead, they are part of much larger groups called galaxies, ranging in size from "small" galaxies (with "only" a million stars or so) all the way up to enormous super-galaxies containing as many as a trillion and spanning more than 100,000 light-years.

Not all galaxies have the same spiral shape as our own Milky Way galaxy, with its bright central nucleus and arms that wind around the nucleus like a pinwheel. Some are elliptical, with very little structure and shapes that range from flat and oval to spherical. Others, called barred spiral galaxies, have arms that extend out from the nucleus in straight lines before trailing off into the pinwheel shape. Still others, called irregular galaxies, tend to be rather small and don't have a symmetrical shape at all.

The Whirlpool galaxy (M51), at left, is a spiral galaxy. It is accompanied by a small, irregular companion galaxy, NGC 5195, at top right. NASA, ESA, S. Beckwith (STScI), and the Hubble Heritage Team (STScI/AURA)

OUR HOME GALAXY: THE MILKY WAY

Like most stars, the Sun belongs to a galaxy. Since the Sun and Earth are embedded in the galaxy, it is difficult for astronomers to obtain an overall view of this galaxy. In fact, what can be seen of its structure is a faint band of stars called the Milky Way (the word *galaxy* comes from the Greek word for "milk"). Because of this, the galaxy has been named the Milky Way galaxy.

The visible band of the Milky Way seems to form a great circle around Earth. This indicates that the galaxy is fairly flat rather than spherical. (If it were spherical, the stars would not be concentrated in a single band.) The Sun is located on the inner edge of a spiral arm. The center, or nucleus, of the galaxy is about 27,000 light-years distant, in the direction of the constellation Sagittarius. All the stars that are visible without a telescope belong to the Milky Way galaxy.

Not all the galaxy's stars are confined to the galactic plane. There are a few stars that occur far above or below the disk. They are usually very old stars, and they form what is called the halo of the galaxy. Evidently the galaxy was originally a roughly spherical mass of gas. Its gravity and rotation caused it to collapse into the disklike shape it has today. The stars that had been formed before the collapse remained in their old positions, but after the collapse further star formation could occur only in the flat disk.

All the stars in the galaxy move in orbits around its center. The Sun takes about 200 million years to complete an orbit. The orbits of most of these stars are nearly circular and are nearly in the same direction. This gives a sense of rotation to the galaxy

The Milky Way galaxy appears as a band in the night sky and is visible to the naked eye.
Kevin Key/Shutterstock.com

as a whole, even as the entire galaxy moves through space.

Dark clouds of dust almost completely obscure astronomers' view of the center of the Milky Way galaxy. Radio waves penetrate the dust, however, so radio telescopes can provide astronomers with a view of the galactic nucleus. In that region stars travel in very fast, tight orbits—which implies the existence of a huge mass at the center. The Earth-orbiting Chandra X-ray Observatory has detected flares of X-rays lasting only a few minutes in the region, which are best explained by the existence of a black hole that is causing the violent acceleration and compression of in-falling blobs of matter. Infrared observations made at the European Southern Observatory (ESO) demonstrated that this supermassive black hole has a mass about 4.3 million times that of the Sun.

ENERGETIC GALAXIES: RADIO GALAXIES AND QUASARS

Galaxies were long thought to be more or less passive objects, containing stars and interstellar gas and dust and shining by the radiation that their stars give off. When astronomers became able to make accurate observations of radio frequencies coming from space, they were surprised to find that a number of galaxies emit large amounts of energy in the radio spectrum. Ordinary stars are so hot that most of their energy is emitted in visible light, with little energy emitted at radio frequencies. Furthermore, astronomers were able to deduce that this radiation had been given off by charged particles of extremely high energy moving in magnetic fields.

How do such galaxies, called radio galaxies, manage to give so much energy to the charged particles and magnetic fields? Radio galaxies are also usually rather peculiar in appearance. Many galaxies, and the radio galaxies in particular, show evidence of interstellar matter expanding away from their centers, as though gigantic explosions had taken place in their

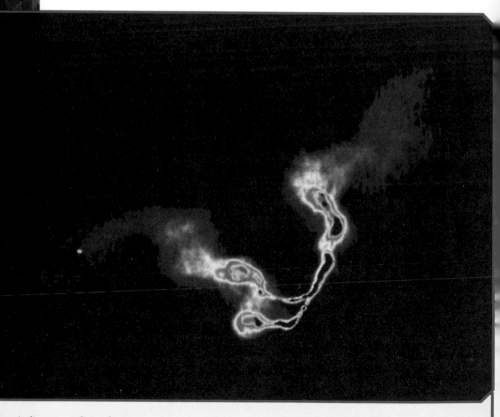

A distant radio galaxy contains two gaseous jets, each emanating from one of the galaxy's twin nuclei. The jets appear to interact and wrap around one another. Courtesy of the National Radio Astronomy Observatory/Associated Universities, Inc.

nuclei. The giant elliptical galaxy known as M87 has a jet of material nearby that it apparently ejected in the past. The jet itself is the size of an ordinary galaxy.

Astronomers have found that, in many galaxies, stars near the center move very rapidly, apparently orbiting some very massive unseen object. The most likely explanation is that a giant black hole, with millions or even billions of times the Sun's mass, lurks in the center of most large galaxies. As stars and gas spiral into these black holes, much of their mass vanishes from sight. The violent heating and compression produces a huge release of energy, including high-speed jets of matter (such as in M87).

Very distant galaxies are sometimes found to have extremely energetic sources of light and radio waves at their centers. These objects, called quasars, are generally believed to be several billion light-years from Earth. This means that astronomers who observe quasars are actually peering several billion years into the past. Most astronomers believe that quasars represent an early phase in the life of some galaxies, when the central black holes, with plenty of fresh gas and stars to consume, were generating huge amounts of energy.

THE QUASAR/GALAXY CONNECTION

A theory astronomers now consider to be likely is that quasars are not actually a separate class of celestial objects as are, say, comets. They are, rather, the bright nuclei of galaxies. In 1943 Carl Seyfert identified a type of galaxy that is spiral in form and has a small, extremely bright nucleus and abnormal spectral features. Some astronomers argue that these galaxies are quasars that are close to the Earth and that other quasars may be the visible nuclei of distant Seyfert galaxies. In 1981 researchers showed that various quasars—including 3C 48, 3C 273, and three others—were in fact embedded in, and probably the nuclei of, galaxies. Although this discovery is very significant, it still does not clarify how quasars or Seyfert galaxies, which are extremely bright, produce their enormous power.

It has also been postulated that quasars may represent galaxies at an early stage of their evolution. Maarten Schmidt found, through study of the red shifts of the known quasars, that the majority of quasars were probably formed not long after (by cosmic standards) the "big bang" that is said to have started the universe. According to this theory these first quasars, which had a brightness a thousand times that of a normal galaxy, have died out, though their light is still seen. It is even possible that many familiar galaxies represent an advanced post-quasar stage.

DARK MATTER

Another problem has puzzled astronomers for years. Most, if not all, galaxies occur in clusters, presumably held together by the gravity of the cluster members. When the motions of the cluster members are measured, however, it is found in almost every case that the galaxies are moving too fast to be held together by only the gravity of the matter that is visible. Astronomers believe there must be a large amount of unseen matter in these clusters— perhaps 10 times as much as can be seen. Although some of this likely consists of objects such as black holes and neutron stars, most of it is believed to be "exotic dark matter," of unknown origin.

THE EXPANDING UNIVERSE

When Albert Einstein published his first cos-mological paper in 1917,

The quasar PKS 2349-014 (bright central disk), several billion light-years from Earth. It appears to be merging with a companion galaxy. John Bahcall, Institute for Advanced Study, NASA

85

he assumed (not being an astronomer) that the universe was static and unchanging. He also assumed that matter was distributed uniformly throughout the universe. But if those assumptions were true, he found, his equations didn't work out: they kept insisting that the mutual gravitation of all the matter in the universe would make it contract—fall in on itself. To get around that problem, Einstein introduced something he called the "cosmological constant," a universal repulsive force that over great distances could counteract the effects of gravity. Once he found out that the universe was not static, but instead was expanding, he described the cosmological constant as the greatest blunder of his career. (It's interesting to note, though, that the cosmological constant has made a reappearance recently in cosmology. Even when he was wrong, Einstein contributed something profound.)

Einstein's equations represented a finite universe that had no edges, because space curved back on itself. In other words, an imaginary traveler in Einstein's universe could travel in a straight line forever and never find the universe's edge, rather like a traveler on earth could travel in a straight line forever and never fall off the edge of the Earth—there is no edge.

At about the time Einstein was working on his cosmological paper, around the beginning of the 20th century, most professional astronomers still believed that the Milky Way was essentially the same thing as the visible universe. Only a minority believed in a theory of island universes—that the spiral nebulae were enormous star systems, much like the Milky Way, scattered through space with vast empty distances between them. One objection to this theory was that very few spiral nebulae could be seen near the plane of the Milky Way, the so-called Zone of Avoidance. That seemed to indicate that the spirals must be associated with the Milky Way. But American astronomer Heber Curtis pointed out that some spirals that can be viewed edge-on obviously contain huge amounts of dust in their "equatorial" planes. If they were similar to the Milky Way, he reasoned, then the Milky Way might also have large amounts of dust throughout its plane, which would block the view of the dim, distant spirals. In 1917 Curtis also found three novae (exploding stars) on his photographs of spirals; the faintness of these novae implied that the spirals were at great distances from the Milky Way.

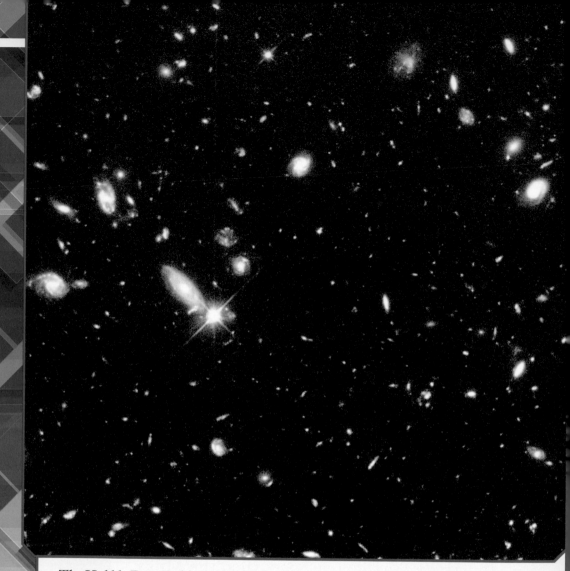

The Hubble Deep Field, a photograph of about 1,500 galaxies, reveals galactic evolution over nearly the entire history of the universe. Robert Williams and the Hubble Deep Field Team (STScI) and NASA

The idea that the universe was static was also being challenged. In 1912, at the Lowell Observatory in Arizona, American astronomer Vesto M. Slipher discovered that light from the Andromeda Nebula (known today as the Andromeda Galaxy) was shifted toward the blue end of the spectrum—an indication that it was moving toward the Milky Way at a speed of up to 200 miles (300 kilometers) per second. That made it the fastest-moving celestial object ever measured at that time.

By 1917 Slipher had measured the speed of some 25 spirals and discovered that some were moving away from the Milky Way as fast as 600 miles (1,000 kilometers) per second. Objects moving at such speeds could hardly belong to the Milky Way. And unlike the Andromeda Nebula, the vast majority of them were moving *away* from the Milky Way: their light was shifted toward the red end of the spectrum. Astronomers did not, however, immediately conclude that the universe is expanding. Because Slipher's spirals were not uniformly distributed around the sky, they instead used the data to try to deduce the velocity of the Sun with respect to the spirals. But Slipher believed that Milky Way itself was a spiral, moving with respect to a greater field of spirals.

In 1917 Dutch mathematician Willem de Sitter found another solution to Einstein's equations that showed a correlation between distance and redshift. Although his solution only worked in a universe devoid of matter, it did motivate astronomers to look for a relationship between distance and redshift. In 1924 Swedish astronomer Karl Lundmark published a study that seemed to show just that. The difficulty was in knowing the distances accurately enough. Lundmark calculated the distance to the Andromeda Nebula by assuming the novae that had been observed there had the same absolute brightness as the ones seen in the Milky Way. Then, for more distant spirals, he assumed they had roughly the same diameter and brightness as the Andromeda Nebula.

On the theoretical side, between 1922 and 1924 Russian mathematician Aleksandr Friedmann studied other solutions to Einstein's equations that allowed expansion or contraction of the universe and, unlike de Sitter's model, also allowed the universe to contain matter. Friedmann's solutions had little immediate impact, partly because of his early death in 1925 and partly because he had not connected his theoretical work with astronomical observations. (It didn't help that Einstein published a note claiming that Friedmann's 1922 paper contained a fundamental error; Einstein later withdrew this criticism.)

CHAPTER 5

THE UNIVERSE

Humans have always wondered about the nature of the universe. How big is it? Does it go on forever, or is there, somewhere, an edge? Has it always been here? If not, how old is it? Is there order to the universe, or is it chaotic? If there is an order to it, has this order always been the same, or has it changed through time?

There also are the questions about our place in the universe. Are we at the center? Does the universe even have a center?

And then there are the questions about the ultimate fate of the universe. Will it go on forever? If not, how will it end? Is it decaying? Still being created? Or perhaps it passes through endless cycles of creation and destruction?

THE NATURE OF THE UNIVERSE

Cosmology is the scientific inquiry into the nature, history, development, and fate

of the universe. By making assumptions that are not contradicted by the behavior of the observable universe, scientists build models, or theories, that attempt to describe the universe as a whole, including its origin and its future. They use each model until something is found that contradicts it. Then the model must be modified or discarded.

Evolutionary Theory of the Universe

Now

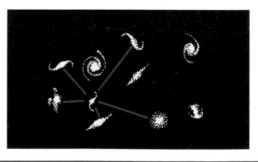

Cosmologists usually assume that, except for small irregularities, the universe has a similar appearance to all observers (and the laws of physics are identical), no matter where in the universe the observers are located or in which direction they look. This unproven concept is called the cosmological principle. One consequence of the cosmological principle is

Billions of Years Later

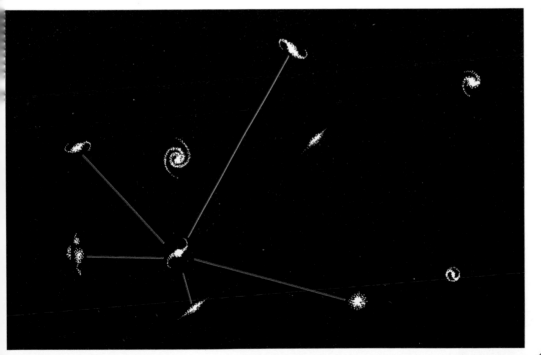

At left is a two-dimensional representation of the universe as it appears now, with galaxies occupying a typical section of space. At right, billions of years later the same amount of matter will fill a larger volume of space. Encyclopædia Britannica, Inc.

that the universe cannot have an edge, for an observer near the edge would have a different view from that of someone near the center. Thus space must be infinite and evenly filled with matter, or the geometry of space must be such that all observers see themselves as at the center. Also, astronomers believe that the only motion that can occur, except for small irregularities, is a uniform expansion or contraction of the universe.

Because the universe appears to be expanding, it seems that it must have been smaller in the past. This is the basis for evolutionary theories of the universe. If one could trace the galaxies back in time, one would find a time at which they were all close together. Observations of the expansion rate indicate that this was between 13 and 14 billion years ago. Thus emerges a picture of an evolving universe that started in some kind of "explosion"—the big bang. Some models of the universe have the expansion continuing forever. Others say that it will stop and be followed by a contraction back to a small volume again. However, data obtained since the late 1990s on the recession speeds of distant supernovae have strongly suggested that the expansion is actually accelerating. This may mean the universe will expand forever. Astronomers are currently

Edwin Hubble. Print Collector/Hulton Archive/Getty Images

trying to explain this acceleration. A current favorite explanation is the idea of dark energy, which might provide a repulsive force that counteracts (and on large scales, overwhelms) the universe's mutual gravitational attraction.

In the 1950s and 1960s there was a rival model, called the steady-state theory. The basic assumption of steady state was a perfect cosmological principle, applying to time as well as position. The steady-state theory stated that the universe must have the same large-scale properties at all times; it cannot evolve, but must remain uniform. Since the universe is seen to be expanding, which would spread the matter out thinner as time goes on, steady-state suggested that new matter must be created to maintain the constant density. In the steady-state theory galaxies are formed, they live and die, and new ones come along to take their places at a rate that keeps the average density of matter constant.

When astronomers observe an object at a great distance, they are seeing it as it looked long ago, because it takes time for light to travel. A galaxy viewed at a distance of a billion light-years is seen as it was a billion years ago. Distant galaxies do seem to be different from nearby galaxies. They seem closer together

LOOKING DEEP: THE HUBBLE SPACE TELESCOPE

The Hubble Space Telescope (HST) is the most sophisticated optical observatory ever placed into orbit around Earth. Named after American astronomer Edwin Hubble, the HST is a large reflecting telescope whose mirror optics gather light from celestial objects and direct it into various recording instruments.

The HST's discoveries have revolutionized astronomy. Observations of Cepheid variables (a type of star whose observed light varies notably in intensity) in nearby galaxies allowed the first accurate determination of Hubble's constant, which is the rate of the universe's expansion. The HST photographed young stars with disks that will eventually become planetary systems. The Hubble Deep Field, a photograph of about 1,500 galaxies, revealed galactic evolution over nearly the entire history of the universe.

than nearby ones, contrary to steady-state contentions but consistent with the view that the universe had a greater density in the past. Also, a faint glow of radiation has been discovered coming uniformly from all directions. Calculations show that this could be radiation left over from the big bang.

HOW THE BIG BANG THEORY WAS DEVELOPED

In 1927 Belgian physicist and cleric Georges Lemaître published a paper in French whose title translated to "A Homogeneous Universe of Constant Mass and Growing Radius, Accounting for the Radial Velocity of the Extragalactic Nebulae."

Lemaître took the Doppler shifts of the spiral nebulae as evidence of a cosmic expansion and used the redshifts and distances of 42 nebulae to deduce a value for the rate of the universe's expansion. At the time, Lemaître's paper had little impact, partly because it had been published in the rather obscure *Annales de la Société Scientifique de Bruxelles* ("Annals of the Scientific Society of Brussels"). It was not fully appreciated until a few years later, when cosmologists and astronomers had become more open to the idea of an expanding universe.

In 1929, building on Friedmann's work, American mathematician and physicist Howard P. Robertson summarized the most general space-time metric (the inherent geometry of space-time) possible assuming that the universe is homogeneous (of the same density everywhere) and isotropic (the same in all spatial directions). Similar results were obtained by English mathematician Arthur G. Walker, so this metric is called the Robertson-Walker metric, and it and the expansion of the universe revealed by the galactic redshifts became the twin foundations of modern cosmology.

HUBBLE PROVES THE ISLAND–UNIVERSE THEORY

In 1923, using the 100-inch (254-cm) reflector telescope at the Mount Wilson Observatory, American astronomer Edwin Hubble identified a Cepheid variable star in the Andromeda Nebula and used that to more precisely measure the distance to the nebula.

Cepheids vary in brightness in a regular and easily identifiable way, with a quick increase in brightness followed by a slower decline. In 1908 American astronomer Henrietta Leavitt had found a relationship between the period and the brightness: the brighter the Cepheid, the longer its period. Ejnar Hertzsprung and American astronomer Harlow Shapley went on to calibrate the relationship in terms of absolute magnitudes: the intrinsic brightness of the star.

Thanks to their work, Hubble was able to determine the Cepheid's absolute magnitude after measuring its period. By comparing that with the observed brightness from Earth, he could calculate how far away the star had to be. This measurement established beyond question that the Andromeda Nebula is outside the Milky Way and is a galaxy in its own right. Further work by Hubble with Cepheid variables in other spiral nebulae confirmed the island-universe theory.

HUBBLE'S LAW

Hubble next turned to the problem of the distance-redshift relationship. In 1929 he published a paper showing a clear linear relationship between distance and redshift, which he interpreted as a velocity. He used Slipher's velocities but incorporated data that had been recorded at Mount Wilson by American astronomer Milton Humason. Distances of the nearer nebulae were found by using Cepheids. At greater distances Hubble used the brightest individual stars that could be resolved, assuming these would be of the same brightness in all galaxies. Even farther out, he used the brightness of the nebula themselves. As a result of his paper, astronomers quickly accepted the distance-redshift (or distance-velocity) relationship. Today, this relationship is known as "Hubble's law."

Hubble was cautious about what the distance-velocity relationship implied about the history of the universe, but the natural conclusion to draw was that at a time in the past all the galaxies had been close together. Because the distance-velocity relationship was linear, if galaxy B was 10 times farther away than galaxy A, it would be receding at 10 times the speed. By the same token, if the galactic clock was run backward to the beginning, both A and B would be at the same point (galaxy B retracing the greater distance at greater speed). Hubble's value for the slope of the line in the velocity-versus-distance graph (today known as the Hubble constant) was 300 miles (500 kilometers) per second per million parsecs (megaparsec). (A parsec is about 3.26 light-years.) With this value for the Hubble constant, the universe appeared to be about two billion years old.

Astronomers later determined that this estimate was far too young. (For example, the study of radioactive isotopes in rocks suggested that Earth had to be 4.5 billion years old, which would make the universe younger than some

of the objects in it!) The value of the Hubble constant has been revised repeatedly. One major correction came in 1952 when American astronomer Walter Baade discovered that Hubble had seriously underestimated galactic distances, because there are actually two different kinds of Cepheids. Baade's recalibration resulted in a halving of the Hubble constant. A further major correction by American astronomer Allan Sandage in 1958 brought it down to about 60 miles (100 km) per second per megaparsec. Sandage, Hubble's former observing assistant, showed that what Hubble had taken as the brightest individual stars in a galaxy were actually tight clusters of bright stars embedded in gaseous nebulae.

For several decades the value of the constant was (according to different researchers) in the range of 30 to 60 miles (50 to 100 km) per second per megaparsec. The currently accepted value for Hubble's constant is around 44 miles (71 km) per second per megaparsec, with a margin of error of about five percent. That, along with many other observations, puts the age of the universe at about 13.7 billion years.

Not everyone accepted that the redshifts were the result of an expanding universe. In 1929 the Swiss astrophysicist Fritz Zwicky proposed that photons gradually give up their energy to the intergalactic matter through which they travel, leading to a progressive reddening of the light. Others simply suggested various versions of the reddening of light with distance (collectively these were called the "tired light" hypothesis) without attempting to provide a physical explanation. These proposals never commanded a wide following, and during the 1930s astronomers and cosmologists increasingly embraced the expansion of the universe.

FIRST HINTS OF THE BIG BANG

The general-relativistic cosmological models and the observed expansion of the universe suggested that the universe was once very small. In the 1930s astronomers began to explore evolutionary models of the universe, a good example being Georges Lemaître's primeval atom. According to Lemaître, the universe began as a single atom having an atomic weight equal to the entire mass of the universe, which then decayed by a super-radiative process until atoms of ordinary atomic weight emerged.

For her doctoral thesis in 1925 British-born American astronomer Cecilia Payne studied the amount of various elements present

in the stars, which can be inferred from the strengths of the absorption lines in the star's spectrum, if these are controlled for the temperature and pressure of the star. One fact that emerged early on was that stars did not have the same composition as Earth and were predominantly hydrogen and helium. In 1938 Norwegian mineralogist Victor Goldschmidt published a detailed summary of data on cosmic abundances of the elements, running over most of the periodic table.

Although Lemaître's theory has some things in common with the big bang theory, it was really a 1948 paper by American physicist Ralph Alpher and his dissertation supervisor, George Gamow, that changed the direction of research by putting nuclear physics into cosmology. As a joke, Gamow added the name of physicist Hans Bethe to the paper so that the sequence of authors—Alpher-Bethe-Gamow—would be an imitation of the first three letters of the Greek alphabet: alpha, beta, gamma (αßγ).

In the αßγ paper, which was only one page long, Alpher and Gamow maintained that the formation of the elements (nucleosynthesis) began about 20 seconds after the start of the expansion of the universe. They supposed that the universe began with a hot dense gas of neutrons, which started to decay into protons and electrons. The building up of the elements was due to successive neutron capture. Using recently published values for the neutron-capture cross-sections of the elements, they integrated their equations to produce a graph of the abundances of all the elements, which resulted in a smooth-curve approximation to the jagged abundance curve that had been published by Goldschmidt.

In another 1948 paper, Alpher and American physicist Robert Herman argued that electromagnetic radiation from the early universe should still exist, but with the expansion should now correspond to a temperature of about 5 K (kelvins, or -268°C [-451°F]) and thus would be visible to radio telescopes.

In a 1953 paper, Alpher, Herman, and American physicist James Follin provided a stage-by-stage history of the early universe, concluding that nucleosynthesis was essentially complete after 30 minutes of cosmic expansion. They deduced that if all the neutrons available at the end of nucleosynthesis went into making helium only, the present-day hydrogen-to-helium ratio would be between 7:1 and 10:1 in terms of numbers of atoms. This would correspond to a present-day universe that was between 29 and 36 percent helium by weight. (Because some neutrons would go into building other elements, the helium figures would be upper limits.) They pointed out that these figures were of the same order as the hydrogen-to-helium ratios measured in planetary nebulae and stellar atmospheres, though these showed quite a large range.

Even though the Gamow-Alpher theory was published in prominent journals and made detailed, testable predictions, it didn't attract a following. The hydrogen-to-helium ratio would not be known precisely enough to test the theory until the 1960s. More crucially, Alpher and Gamow failed to interest radio astronomers in looking for the background radiation. As a result, their prediction was soon forgotten.

THE STEADY-STATE CHALLENGE

The same year the αßγ paper came out, 1948, a new theory appeared in England: the steady-state universe. Different versions of it were proposed by English

Fred Hoyle. London Daily Express/ Pictorial Parade

mathematician and astronomer Fred Hoyle and by the team of British mathematician and cosmologist Hermann Bondi and British astronomer Thomas Gold, but the key idea was that although the universe was expanding, its average properties did not change with time. According to the theory, as the universe expanded the density of matter did not diminish because new hydrogen atoms were created that formed clouds of gas that condensed into new stars and galaxies. The number of new hydrogen atoms required per year was so tiny that one could not hope to observe this process directly.

However, there were predictable observational consequences that would make it possible to distinguish between a steady-state universe or a big bang universe. (The term *big bang* was coined in a radio talk in 1949 by Hoyle as a way to poke mild fun at the rival theory.) For example, in a big bang universe, when one looks at galaxies that are far away, one also sees them as they were in the remote past (because of the travel time of the light). Thus, one might expect that distant galaxies are less-evolved or that they contain more young stars. But in a steady-state universe, one would see galaxies at all possible stages of evolutionary development at even the farthest distances.

The density of galaxies in space should also diminish with time in a big bang universe. Therefore, galaxies at great distances should be more densely crowded together than nearby galaxies are. But in a steady-state universe, the average density of galaxies should be about the same everywhere and at every time. In the 1950s the Cambridge radio astronomer Martin Ryle showed that there were more radio galaxies at great distances than there were nearby, thus showing that the universe had evolved over time, a result that could not be explained in steady-state theory.

The discovery of quasars (quasi-stellar radio sources) in the early 1960s also showed the steady-state theory less likely to be true. Quasars were first identified as strong radio sources that in visible light appear to be identified with small starlike objects. Further, they have large redshifts, which implies that they are very far away. From their distance and their apparent luminosity, it was inferred that they emit enormous amounts of energy; a single quasar might be brighter than a whole galaxy. There was no room for such objects in a steady-state universe, in which the contents of any region of space (seen as it is now or as it was long ago) should be roughly similar. The quasars were a clear sign that the universe was evolving.

Steady-state theory never had a large following, and its supporters were centered in Britain. Nevertheless, having a competing theory forced the big bang cosmologists to strengthen their arguments and to collect supporting data. A key question centered on the abundances and origins of the chemical elements. In steady-state theory, it was essential that all the elements could be synthesized in stars. By contrast, in the aßγ paper, Alpher and Gamow tried to show that all the elements could be made in the big bang. Of course, in a more reasonable view, big bang theorists had to accept that some element formation does take place in stars, but they were keen to show that the stars could not account for all of it. In particular, the stars could not be the source of most of the light elements. For example, it was impossible to see how during the lifetime of a galaxy the stars could build up the helium content to 30 percent.

In 1957 Hoyle, with American astronomers William Fowler, Margaret Burbidge, and Geoffrey Burbidge (or B^2FH, as their paper was later called), gave a detailed account of the abundances of most elements in terms of

conditions appropriate to stellar interiors. The paper was often seen as favoring the steady-state model because it had not made use of temperature and pressure conditions appropriate to the big bang. But in later papers (in 1964 with English astrophysicist Roger Tayler and 1967 with Fowler and American physicist Robert Wagoner), Hoyle concluded that the lighter elements could be built up satisfactorily only in conditions like those of the big bang. Hoyle himself continued to favor supermassive objects as the origin of the elements, but most astronomers saw his work as vindicating the big bang theory.

When good estimates of the cosmic abundance of deuterium and other light elements became available, the big bang theory proved capable of detailed explanation of the cosmic abundances of all the light elements. According to current thinking, most of the heavier elements were then built up in stars and supernova explosions.

COSMIC MICROWAVE BACKGROUND PROVES THE THEORY

In 1965 American astronomers Arno Penzias and Robert W. Wilson were working at Bell

Robert W. Wilson and Arno Penzias. Ted Thai/Time & Life Pictures/Getty Images

Laboratories on a 20-foot (6-meter) horn antenna. The original purpose of the antenna was to detect reflected signals from high-altitude balloons, with the goal of applying the technology to communications satellites, but Penzias and Wilson had adapted it for doing radio astronomy. They detected a constant, persistent signal, corresponding to an excess temperature of 3.3 K (-269.9°C [-453.7°F]). After eliminating every source of circuit noise they could think of, and even shooing a pair of pigeons that had been roosting (and

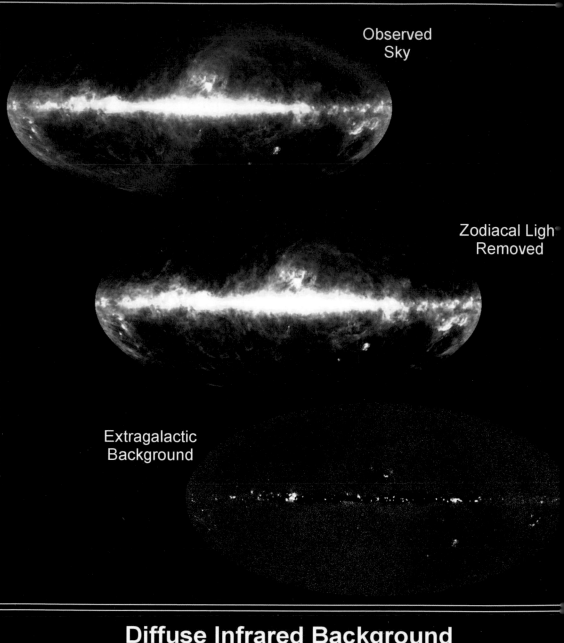

Observed
Sky

Zodiacal Light
Removed

Extragalactic
Background

Diffuse Infrared Background
COBE • DIRBE

Three views of the infrared universe by the Cosmic Background Explorer (COBE) satellite. Evidence from COBE's investigation of the universe's cosmic microwave background (CMB) supports the big bang theory. Photo AURA/STScI/NASA/ JPL (NASA photo # STScI-PRC98-01) leaving behind "white dielectric material") in the horn, they found that the signal remained and that it was constant, no matter in which direction the telescope was pointed. At nearby Princeton University, they consulted with American physicist Robert Dicke, who was studying oscillatory models of the universe with hot phases and who was therefore not surprised by what they had found.

About the same time, astrophysicist James Peebles, Dicke's former student, also published a paper predicting the existence of a universal background radiation at a temperature of 10 K (-263°C [-441°F]), apparently completely unaware of Alpher and Herman's earlier prediction. Suddenly the pieces fell together. The cosmic microwave background (CMB) was accepted as the third major piece of evidence in support of the big bang theory.

In the early stages of the expansion, when atoms were all still completely ionized, the universe was opaque to electromagnetic radiation. But when the universe cooled enough to allow the formation of neutral atoms, it suddenly became transparent to electromagnetic radiation (just as light can travel through air). At this "decoupling time," the electromagnetic radiation was of very high energy and very

short wavelengths. With the continued expansion of space, wavelengths were stretched until they reached their current microwave lengths (from about a millimeter to tens of centimeters in wavelength). Thus, every bit of empty space acts as a source of radio waves—a phenomenon predicted (twice!) by the big bang theory but for which steady-state theory had no ready explanation. For most cosmologists, this marked the end of the steady-state theory, even though Hoyle and his collaborators continued to tweak and adjust the theory to try to meet objections.

By the mid-1960s, the big bang theory had become the standard cosmology, underpinned by the observed expansion, the measured abundances of the light elements, and the presence of the cosmic microwave background.

CONCLUSION

The goal of astronomy has always been to look deeper and deeper into Earth's tantalizing night sky, to tease out its hidden secrets despite the enormous distances separating us from even the nearest of our celestial neighbors. Today's technology, from orbiting telescopes to powerful computers running sophisticated models, has given modern astronomers unprecedented tools for unlocking the mysteries of the universe.

We know the age of the universe. We have a good idea of how it all began (with a violent explosion) and how stars, planets, and galaxies formed. We have learned an enormous amount about our planetary neighbors and we know a great deal about the stars we share with the Milky Way.

Despite the fact that so much is known, we continue to learn more. Not that many years ago, we didn't know for certain if there were any planets orbiting other stars. Now we know that planets are everywhere. Soon we may know if some of those planets are capable of sustaining life—or even confirm that life is there.

The universe is unimaginably large—and yet, thanks to the science of astronomy, we can imagine it: imagine what might be in it and design tools to help us find out if we're right.

And we don't have to just imagine. Because of developments of satellites and telescopes, we can actually see what space looks like. Stunning photographs of nebulae and galaxies far away give all of us an idea of what's out there. Although space images seem like the set of a science fiction movie, even the average person now understands what scientists are studying.

Astronomy may be the oldest science of all, but as the 21st century advances, one thing is certain: it will continue to surprise us.

asteroid Any of the thousands of small rocky celestial bodies that circle around the Sun.

black hole A celestial object that has a gravitational field so strong that light cannot escape it.

celestial Of or relating to the sky or visible heavens.

comet A celestial body that typically has a highly eccentric orbit and when relatively near the Sun appears as a fuzzy object with one or more long tails.

dark matter Nonluminous matter not yet directly detected by astronomers that is hypothesized to exist to account for various observed gravitational effects.

eclipse The total or partial obscuring of one celestial body by another.

electromagnetic radiation Energy that travels in the form of an electromagnetic wave (as a radio wave, wave of visible light, or X-ray) and that has both electrical and magnetic components and moves at a speed of about 186,000 miles (300,000 kilometers) per second.

galaxy Any of the very large groups of stars and associated matter that are found throughout the universe.

light-year The distance that light travels within a vacuum in one year—about 5.88 trillion miles (9.46 trillion kilometers).

magnitude A number representing the intrinsic or apparent brightness of a celestial body on a logarithmic scale in which an increase of one unit corresponds to a reduction in the brightness of light by a factor of 2.512.

moon A large round natural object that orbits a planet.

nebula A cloud of gas or dust in space; also a group of stars that are very far away and look like a bright cloud.

neutron star A dense celestial object that consists primarily of closely packed neutrons and that results from the collapse of a much larger stellar body.

nova A star that suddenly increases its light output tremendously and then fades away to its former obscurity in a few months or years.

parallax In astronomy, the angular difference in direction of a celestial body as measured from two points on Earth's orbit.

parsec A unit of astronomical distance that is based on parallax and equal to a distance of 19.2 trillion miles (30.9 trillion kilometers).

planet A large, round object that orbits a star.

quasar A very bright object in space that has the appearance of a star but is beyond the Milky Way galaxy and is a strong emitter of radio waves.

radio telescope A piece of equipment that receives radio waves from space and that is used for finding stars and other objects.

spectrograph An instrument for dispersing radiation (such as electromagnetic radiation or sound waves) into a spectrum and recording or mapping the spectrum.

star A self-luminous, gaseous celestial body of great mass that produces energy by means of a type of nuclear reaction called fusion.

supernova An exploding star that can temporarily become as much as a billion times brighter than the Sun.

telescope An optical instrument for viewing distant objects by means of the refraction of light rays through a lens or the reflection of light rays by a concave mirror.

variable star A star whose brightness changes, typically over fairly regular intervals of time.

FOR MORE INFORMATION

American Astronomical Society
2000 Florida Avenue NW, Suite 300
Washington, DC 20009-1231
(202) 328-2010
Website: http://www.aas.org
The American Astronomical Society (AAS)
 is the major organization of professional
 astronomers in North America. Its mission is to enhance and share humanity's
 scientific understanding of the universe.

Association of Universities for Research in
 Astronomy
1212 New York Avenue NW, Suite 450
Washington, DC 20005
(202) 483-2101
Website: http://www.aura-astronomy.org
The Association of Universities for
 Research in Astronomy (AURA) is a
 consortium of 39 U.S. institutions and
 6 international affiliates that operates
 world-class astronomical observatories.
 AURA's role is to establish, nurture,
 and promote public observatories and
 facilities that advance innovative astronomical research. In addition, AURA is

deeply committed to public and educational outreach and to diversity throughout the astronomical and scientific workforce.

Astronomical League
9201 Ward Parkway, Suite 100
Kansas City, MO 64114
(816) 333-7759
Website: http://www.astroleague.org
The Astronomical League is an umbrella organization of amateur astronomy societies. Currently their membership consists of over 240 organizations across the United States, along with a number of members-at-large, patrons, and supporting members. The mission of the Astronomical League is to promote astronomy, through encouraging public interest via local astronomy clubs.

Planetary Society
85 South Grand Avenue
Pasadena, CA 91105
(626) 793-5100
Website: http://www.planetary.org
The Planetary Society was founded in 1980 by Carl Sagan, Bruce Murray, and Louis Friedman to inspire and involve

the world's public in space exploration through advocacy, projects, and education. Today, the Planetary Society is the largest and most influential organization that is focused on space and open to the public.

Royal Astronomical Society of Canada
203-4920 Dundas Street W
Toronto, ON M9A 1B7
Canada
(888) 924-7272 (in Canada)
(416) 924-7973
Website: http://www.rasc.ca
The Royal Astronomical Society of Canada
    is a national, nonprofit, charitable organi-
    zation devoted to the advancement of
    astronomy and related sciences. It has 29
    local branches and about 4,200 members
    worldwide.

SETI Institute
189 Bernardo Avenue, Suite 100
Mountain View, CA 94043
(650) 961-6633
Website: http://www.seti.org
The SETI Institute is a private, nonprofit
    organization whose mission is to explore,
    understand, and explain the origin, nature,

and prevalence of life in the universe. The institute has three centers, the Center for SETI Research, the Carl Sagan Center for the Study of Life in the Universe, and the Center for Education and Public Outreach. Founded in November 1984, the SETI Institute employs more than 120 scientists, educators, and support staff.

WEBSITES

Because of the changing nature of Internet links, Rosen Publishing has developed an online list of websites related to the subject of this book. This site is updated regularly. Please use this link to access the list:

http://www.rosenlinks.com/SCI/Astro

FOR FURTHER READING

Comins, Neil F. *About the Universe.* 8th ed. New York, NY: W.H. Freeman & Company, 2008.

Dickinson, Terence. *Nightwatch: A Practical Guide to Viewing the Universe.* 4th ed. Richmond Hill, ON: Firefly Books, 2006.

Graham, Ian, and Geriant H. Jones, M.D. *Exploring Science: Space.* Mountain View, CA: Armadillo Press, 2014.

Ishikawa, Kenji. *The Manga Guide to the Universe.* San Francisco, CA: No Starch Press, 2011.

Lippincott, Kristen. *Astronomy.* New York, NY: DK Publishing, 2008.

Moche, Dinah L. *Astronomy: A Self-Teaching Guide.* 7th ed. Hoboken, NJ: Wiley & Sons, 2009.

Perricone, Mike. *The Big Bang.* New York, NY: Chelsea House, 2009.

Rey, H.A. *The Stars: A New Way to See Them.* 2nd ed. Boston, MA: HMH Books for Young Readers, 2008.

Ritter, Gordon. *Planets, Stars, and Galaxies.* New York, NY: Facts on File, 2007.

Schaaf, Fred. *Seeing the Sky: 100 Projects, Activities & Explorations in Astronomy.* Mineola, NY: Dover Publications, 2012.